JOHN HENRY MARTIN

is currently chairman of the U.S. Office of Education's task force on the reform of American high schools. A former teacher, principal, superintendent of schools, visiting professor, and corporation executive, Dr. Martin is a consultant to schools and industry and author of numerous articles and studies of children and education.

CHARLES H. HARRISON

is director of Communications Services, has served as a consultant/writer for the U.S. Office of Education and the Ford Foundation, and was education editor of New Jersey's largest evening newspaper. A contributor to numerous magazines, Mr. Harrison was cited by the New Jersey Education Association for "his editorial integrity and educational insight."

FREE TO LEARN

Unlocking and Ungrading American Education

JOHN HENRY MARTIN & CHARLES H. HARRISON

A SPECTRUM BOOK

Prentice-Hall, Inc., *Englewood Cliffs, New Jersey*

Library of Congress Cataloging in Publication Data

MARTIN, JOHN HENRY.
    Free to learn.

    (A Spectrum book)
    Includes bibliographical references.
    1. Education–U. S.–1965-   I. Harrison.
Charles Hampton   joint author. II. Title.
LA210.M33   370'.973   72–672
ISBN 0–13–331066–3
ISBN 0–13–331058–2 (pbk.)

10   9   8   7   6   5   4   3

Prentice-Hall International, Inc. (London)
Prentice-Hall of Australia, Pty. Ltd. (Sydney)
Prentice-Hall of Canada, Ltd. (Toronto)
Prentice-Hall of India Private Limited (New Delhi)
Prentice-Hall of Japan, Inc. (Tokyo)

Contents

v

Prologue

THIS BOOK WAS BORN shortly after the death in 1965–66 of a long-established faith in the panaceas for educational reform developed, endorsed, and taught by the teachers' colleges and leaders of the American educational establishment.

Two years before its untimely death, the faith had been sacred to us, keeping company in our soul with such noble faiths as those that trusted in the rightness of the Golden Rule and the Declaration of Independence.

We had been party to a miracle worked in a city school system when the board of education and the people of that city agreed to increase the school budget by 35 percent.

All the money was dedicated to putting into practice the tenets of the faith that had been preached so eloquently and accepted so trustingly from prestigious graduate school of education to state teachers' college. Millions were spent on a series of things that were assumed to be the keys to quality education.

- Class size was reduced from an average of just over thirty to an average of just over twenty.
- More specialists of every description were hired. There were more guidance personnel, more psychologists and social workers, more classroom aides, and more remedial teachers. In fact, two full-time remedial reading teachers were assigned to *each* of the elementary schools, where the average enrollment was 600.

1

- More teachers with advanced degrees were hired.
- Modern math, modern physics, and advanced courses were given priority status in the all-out drive to raise the achievement level for all children—black and white, poor and rich.
- An incredible five out of every six teachers were engaged in retraining programs of one kind or another. It was a phenomenal effort to prepare the staff to handle innovations that were great in number.
- More than sixty curricular and teaching reforms were initiated.
- A dynamic teachers' council, elected by secret ballot, sat in review and control over the superintendent's recommendations to the board of education.

But when all the tenets of the faith had been in practice for two years, a suspicion grew that the stupendous investment might not be paying off. A first-rate psychometrician—one of the best in the country—was employed to test the suspicion. The examination was painstakingly thorough and exceptionally sophisticated.

First students were measured for basic academic achievement. Then these results were cross-referenced against such factors as class size, age of the teacher, teacher experience, and students' race, sex, and family income.

In the end, the cherished faith died. The psychometrician filed an expert and precise report that said in effect: "The millions have purchased no measurable change in student achievement; all that was done to make a difference has made *no* difference." The panaceas were, after all, only false promises—vain expectations. All the patented prescriptions for high student achievement that made such a grand appearance in the college textbooks and the theses of the pedagogues had failed the hard test of reality in the field.

Anticipating the much-heralded Coleman Report by one year, the study showed that small classes, older and more experienced teachers with advanced degrees, more specialists—all the things that more money could buy—did not improve education when measured by children's scores on tests in reading, language development, and arithmetic.

We began to pick our brains for a clue to the causes of the fiasco. Working many times faster than the fastest computer, we raced back through perhaps a billion things remembered to the middle thirties and memories of a one-room school in rural Alabama. We even recalled how the kids were sewn into red flannels at the first hard frost, and how they emerged at the thaw seeming to be something less pristine than butterflies.

The War between the States was just yesterday outside Tuscaloosa. King Cotton lay rotting in the fields and poverty ruled the land.

Sometimes there was public schooling, but it was on the verge of not existing at all. The going rate in Alabama for a teacher with a college degree was sixty-five dollars a month, but in the farmland seven miles from the University of Alabama even that sum of money wasn't available. There were scant public funds for teachers or for textbooks, and whatever books there were for children had to be bought out of the meager generosity of the few persons who had a little more than their neighbors.

Into this land came a stranger from the university—a Yankee, of all things. But he was learning to be a teacher. Besides, he told the school trustee who also ran *the* store in those parts, he would come around from time to time and dispense learning for the nonsalary then being offered by the board of education. So, perhaps reluctantly, he was hired.

When later he walked those long seven miles out of the twentieth-century town into nineteenth-century ruralism, and while he was yet away off from the one-room school, the bell cord was pulled. The students came from as far away as the sound of the bell would carry, and the bell tolled for seven-year-olds and fourteen-year-olds and all the year-olds in between. When the weather was good and there was farm work to be done or hooky to be played, attendance might reach twenty-five. But in bad weather, fifty children might fill the building.

Now, these rustics living in a bygone day in a bygone land found it necessary to teach the Yankee teacher how to teach. From their benches they instructed: "We study a subject in our form. When you call for a form to recite, those of us in that form stand forward. You record a mark for the recitation, and then that form stands down. Here, we'll show you what we mean. Call for the fourth form in geography." He did, and a small group of kids of different ages came forward. He heard their recitation and recorded a mark for each one.

"Now, call for the fourth form in spelling." Of course, there were giggles from some as the instruction of the teacher continued. He called for the fourth form in spelling. About half of those in the fourth form for geography sat down, their places being taken by other children of varied ages. Then they recited and had marks put down by their names.

And so the teaching went in the one room of the one-room school district in old-fashioned America. The children studied at their benches, sharing the scarce books and tutoring one another. If they needed help, they went to someone in a higher form, who might be older or younger, or they came to the teacher. If the teacher wanted to demonstrate long division to those who were ready for it, he collected them around the slate board and explained the mysteries in conversational tones. But off to the side, openly eavesdropping, would be a gaggle of children who wanted either to move ahead to long division or to catch up on it.

What the Yankee would-be-teacher was learning, of course, was what mankind—particularly children—always has known. *Each child differs from every other child, and some children are more intelligent than others. Furthermore, every child is brighter in some things than he is in others.* Hell, he might be in the fourth form for arithmetic, but in the seventh form for reading. These truths are as old and self-evident as the hills of New England and the flatlands of the Midwest. The kids knew these truths well enough to impart them to a greenhorn teacher, and they would have laughed him out of their school if he had been silly enough to suggest that all nine-year-olds should stand forward to recite the same lesson in geography. "But," the nine-year-olds would have protested, "we don't know the same thing; we don't learn at the same time or in the same way. Gee, can't you see that?"

Looking back from a distance of thirty years, suddenly we did see. The institutional form of the one-room school was radically different from the institutional form of the school where children and subject matter are sorted into grades. Each form imposes its own behaviors on teachers and students. The one-room school forced the teacher to cater to the differences among children and the differences within each child. But the graded school requires that the teacher stand before his class of same-year-olds and teach whatever sameness has been prescribed for children in his grade.

We now saw that the total design of the institution into which the city school system had so recently pumped millions of dollars worth of guaranteed reforms without effect was terribly wrong. Massive attempts to enhance the learning of individual students had been made in an institution designed for instruction of the masses. They had to fail.

We realized that the wise men whose wisdom we had revered were in fact schizophrenic. In their imaginings, the rhetoric that only described an intent to do good things for individual children had been transformed into real accomplishments.

They had advocated reducing class size, for example, because it was commonsense logic. If the teacher had twenty children instead of thirty, they reasoned, why naturally she could teach individuals better. But the logic was shattered in the institution that was designed for and committed to mass education in twelve separate grade packages. And while the teacher was more comfortable with twenty children than with thirty, while she was able to control twenty children better than thirty, *the twenty children didn't learn one bit better than the thirty children when the teacher taught the twenty with the same methods used for the thirty.*

The explosive recognition that the one-room school was a social institution which shaped an appropriate set of teaching methods and that the graded school required contrary learning patterns led to five years of further study of institutional behavior in schools here and abroad. A series of hypotheses were developed that form the basis for this book.

It became increasingly apparent that when there is a mismatch between an institution's structure and its avowed purposes, dysfunctioning occurs. The symptoms of this pathology became evident as schools were observed. Among these symptoms are the following:

- The use of flamboyant rhetoric to describe the schools' purposes.
- The vast gulf between goals and the schools' outcomes.
- Job descriptions not matched by tasks performed.
- A dichotomy keeping these discrepancies sufficiently separated so that neither individuals nor the institution find them in conflict.
- A compulsive consensus—an ideological conformity.
- Hypertrophy, the proliferation of functions.
- A strange mix of group defensiveness with acceptance of the role of the school as the savior of society, the answer to all ills.

One of the first characteristics of an educational institution whose fit to its purposes is skewed is the fancy rhetoric used to describe its goals. The prose style resembles the language of evangelical theology. The results of every curriculum are hyperbole and perfection. Children are to be transformed into superb mathematicians, paragons of civic virtue, masters of language in writing and speech, social problem-solvers, and culturally sensitive users and creators of the arts.

The language used to describe the goals of teaching nine-year-olds in the fourth grade differs little from what we would expect from a utopian view of the perfectibility of man.

And the users of the language seem to be unaware of the gulf between the description of desired outcomes and the real accomplishments of children. Contradictorily, the awareness of the gap is acute. But what is missing is a sense of institutional responsibility for the gap. The learner is blamed for falling short; fault is found with his genes, home, community, or the outlook of his generation. Accordingly, the institution credits itself with the highest of goals. Indeed, it is driven to elevate them above criticism to compensate for the defensive feelings of inadequacy its members feel in the face of depressing realities.

Golden promises and tarnished results are not unique to schools. But the glitter of the language can be useful as an index of the institution's dysfunctioning. It is tempting to describe this as schizoid behavior. But there seems to be no trauma when there exists no conscious or unconscious awareness of the gulf between the words of the schools' goals and the realities of the outcomes. A compartmented dichotomy characterizes an educational institution whose structure is ill-designed for its purposes.

Another symptom of structural weakness in the schools is the hidden inadequacy of task review, performance criteria, and the whole series of functions under the heading of foremanship and supervision. One aspect of this which fills the literature is the plea for the building principal to perform these supervisory roles.

The almost universal noncompliance of most principals with these functions is assumed to be the difference among individuals. That is, "good" principals perform supervisory functions, including classroom visitations and individual teacher conferences, while "poor" principals neglect these functions.

What is not seen is that the institution's requirements of the principal diverge from the paper description of his position. And under these conditions the institution's nonfunctioning standards will be obeyed most of the time.

Also characteristic of poorly organized institutions is the need for and the existence of consensus. School people are expected to believe the same thing and to express the same point of view about reading methods, grading systems, reporting procedures, the place of science in the elementary school, language laboratories, and why the school or school district has adopted or rejected the latest reform. It is no matter whether the reform is a new version of modern math or the need to reorganize the junior high school into a four-year middle school.

But the substance of the consensus is not of significance. What is significant—and frightening—is the universality of its occurrence. It is remarkable and relatively unique to find faculties of schools divided on these issues. Communities may be, but teachers seldom are.

Fostering this condition are such anachronisms as dictatorial administrative styles that are long out of date and now rapidly disappearing under the pressure of teacher militancy. Thus the institution has shifted the control agent from the school administrator to the teacher organization, while conformity as an institutional way of life continues.

Still another factor contributing to this phenomenon of ideological conformity is the institution's chronic defensive posture requiring internal agreement as the price of status in the group.

An additional symptom of structural defect in our schools is the phenomenon that the biologists and cultural anthropologists call hypertrophy. Hypertrophy is an inexplicable event associated with the closing phases in the evolution of an animal. After the animal has reached the climax of its development, it tends to proliferate nonfunctional characteristics that hasten the extinction of the species. In the case of the American graded school this has been accompanied by an insatiable appetite for new functions.

Every discovery of a societal deficiency becomes the generative source for adding specially titled new personnel to the institution. Delinquency, drugs, divorce, voter apathy, slums, poverty, civil rights, highway safety, alcoholism, crime, tooth decay, racism, and pollution all have been and are being used as justification for the continual accretion of new posts, programs, courses, and costs.

It is an unfortunate truth of our culture that we accept the proposition that schools—"good" schools—can teach anything, right all wrongs, subdue any evil. And our schools, poorly organized even for the learning of the three R's, accept the impossible assignments. For example, we believe the schools can change racial attitudes of our society. This faith in the potency of education ought not to blind us to the evidence that cultural values are taught by many other institutions in addition to the school and in many other ways than formal education.

The danger of this faith is in its excessive reliance upon the schools for a goal which they can only approximate. If an educational objective is narrow in the life of a student and only of minor consequence to the welfare of the state, the quality of the schools' output will not generate great anxiety. But if, as in the case of racial peace, the objective is vital to the survival of society, then the overestimate of the schools' competence is an exercise in domestic brinkmanship.

In chapter 7 we describe how, with Madison Avenue as a paraprofessional, the schools taught cleanliness. But when advertising taught otherwise, the schools accomplished little in their campaign to wipe out smoking and alcoholism.

We need to recognize that as a society we educate through other methods and institutions than formal education in the schools. We educate through child-rearing techniques, radio, television, press, films, magazines, music and lyrics, the pulpit, and in taxicabs and beauty parlors—to name a few of the media. Education must not be seen as the exclusive responsibility of schools, and schools must not be seen as the only means for education.

Children and adults learn in many differing ways. Variety in the social forms of education are needed to fit human diversity. We describe new ways to legislate educational variety and create new means and institutions for guidance, physical education and health, the arts, and vocational education.

In each of the first six chapters we apply the insights of these concepts as ways of looking at existing practices, programs, and organizations in the schools. Taking major elements of the graded school, we test them for the incidence of dysfunctioning. Then in each chapter we propose a new institution designed to function productively and in harmony with its purposes. In the last two chapters we describe a broad range of ideas, practices, organizations, and techniques that the dynamic push of our hypotheses has generated, as well as those current innovations in need of a conceptual home that won't distort them or thrust them out.

We have conceived a new Design for Community Education—a way to unlock and ungrade American education so that individuals are free to learn.

This book blends the new insights and basic concepts for change in American education conceived by John Henry Martin with the observations and literary style of Charles H. Harrison. Immodestly, we believe the collaboration has been productive.

We deliberately eschewed voluminous footnotes and bibliography —the traditional trademarks of scholarship. We did so because it is our intent to clearly inform and dramatically move all Americans —laymen and professional educators—to free American education from the straitjackets imposed by dysfunctioning institutions.

Finally, while we have found the structure of the graded school to be unsound, we have labored hard—and we think successfully— to keep ourselves from falling headlong into that rut which over- flows with critics who blame the institution's weaknesses and failings on those who are only victimized by the institution.

One

From Prussia with Locks

ONCE UPON A TIME America decided its children should learn how to read and write and cipher.

And the children were brought together for the learning in a place called a school.

And the school was one room.

And in that room were boys and girls. Some were almost babies and some were almost men and women; some were very bright and some were not bright at all.

After a while there were too many children for the one room, so other rooms were added. Then there were too many children for one school, so other schools were added.

Because there were so many children and so many rooms and schools, the managers of education decided to reorganize the process by which children learned how to read and write and cipher.

But a great blunder was made.

The managers of education borrowed from Prussia the idea of packaging children into grades according to their age. Children aged six went into the first grade, children aged seven went into the second grade, and so on. To make things even simpler—from a managerial point of view—whatever there was to know about reading, writing, and ciphering was put into one-year packages. Six-year-olds in the first grade were taught just so much and no more; seven-year-olds in the second grade picked up where the six-year-olds left off. And so it went, the idea being that it would con-

11

tinue until the schools either ran out of grades or something to teach, whichever came soonest.

Back in the days when the school was one room, everybody inside those four plain walls knew what mankind always had known. *Each child differs from every other child, and some children are more intelligent than others. Furthermore, every child is brighter in some things than he is in others.* The one-room teacher, faced by a mixed bag of children aged seven to seventeen, could not possibly do otherwise than to teach different materials differently to each student.

But under the new organization the teacher was expected to stand before his class of same-year-olds and teach whatever sameness had been prescribed for children in his grade. The blunder was that the facade of sameness created by age and grade only masked the real differences that still existed among the children.

Today's second grade still calls for second-year reading instruction—whatever has been packaged for seven-year-olds. There exists in every second grade in the United States, however, a child who only was confused by introductory reading instruction in the previous year, a child who learned to read before he ever entered school, and all the other youngsters in between those extremes. The curriculum is still packaged for instruction despite the evidence that decades of graded lessons have failed to reach or teach the great diversity among children even of the same age.

Since the turn of the century, even as the graded and packaged institution was denying the old truths about human differences, the psychologists were rediscovering these ancient truths that were nourished in the old one-room school.

And this rediscovery of children's differences as new *scientific* truths began to affect teacher training. So, for at least seventy years, America's educators have been struggling to provide individualized education in an institution that makes individualized education almost impossible. One reform after another has tried to revamp the curriculum, rewrite materials, introduce television and computers, retrain teachers, provide a combination of everything. We have tried homogeneous grouping, tracking, and honors courses.

But the reform always has been defeated by the system it has come to as a friend. It is as though the reform were a foreign heart sewn into a body that needs it desperately. Despite the body's need and the brain's conscious gratitude for the help, all of the body's juices unconsciously and automatically conspire against the new heart. Ultimately, the organ is overwhelmed and killed, or damaged sufficiently so that its effectiveness is sharply reduced.

Reformers have seen the graded school system only as classrooms of children, each room directed by a teacher, each school directed by a principal, all schools directed by a superintendent, and the whole works governed by a board of education. What they have failed to see is that the school system is also a social system, where people behave toward each other and toward everything that happens within the institution according to the rules and roles inherent to the form of the system.

And so one reform demonstrates how students benefit from frequent and open sharing of ideas, questions, and problems with their teachers and with each other. But the system, because it was designed to control masses, orders students to be seen but not heard, except in guarded and guided response to teachers' questions. The system rewards those teachers who keep their students busy and quiet at their desks and rewards that principal who can prove that the only hum in his building emanates from the boiler room.

And another reform shows that students can learn much and learn it better through independent study in a well-equipped resource center. But the system long ago required that every teacher must always know the whereabouts of every student for whom he is responsible and know what each is doing at any given moment. The system makes teachers reluctant to allow a student to leave the room to go to the toilet, let alone the resource center. The system does not look favorably upon teachers whose students are frequently walking the halls when they should be in class sitting quietly.

To the architect, the form of structure is dictated by the function to be performed inside the structure. But in the social organizations called institutions, the functions performed by those inside the institution are dictated by the form or nature of the institution.

Consider the functions dictated by the one-room school compared to the functions dictated by the graded school.

In the one-room school, older children managed younger children as they did—and still do—in every neighborhood, in large families, and in children's play not controlled by adults. Children in the one-room school expected each other to lead, direct, help, carry, follow, and ask. These relationships seemed natural to them, but it was only because the form of the social group—the school—nudged them into these behaviors.

In the graded school, where classrooms contained children of nearly the same age, children's expectations of each other changed. Such simple measures of each other as bigger and older could no longer be applied. The organization of the group became difficult and unsettled because the children had to work out new relationships.

The group that once knew how to work and play together now found itself asking such polarizing questions as these: "Who is smartest?" "In what?" "Who is fastest, prettiest, best dressed?" "Who is the teacher's favorite?" "Who is strongest, the best climber?" And for each of these questions there were the answers by which the group determined who was slowest, ugliest, and the fattest.

In the one-room school the need to judge and rank was reduced and quickly accomplished. The resulting stability relaxed the children. They knew they belonged to the group. But when children were organized into grades the institution inadvertently increased their need to judge and rank each other. The result was friction and instability.

The teacher in the one-room school did not find it upsetting or complicated to manage the group. The group was largely self-managing. And if the instructional patterns imposed by the teacher did not seriously disrupt the relations between children, the class operated rather calmly and orderly.

But the graded school, where children were confused and made tense by the necessity to invent new and unnatural relationships, required the teacher to manage an unstable climate with great skill and strength. The group, lacking now the internal controls it had in the one-room school, needed the teacher to impose order.

Another effect upon the behavior of children impelled by the form of the group, or institution, is that the one-room school made the act of helping each other seem natural. In fact, the early versions of the institution sat children in pairs or, in the case of the youngest children, on benches built for three.

But asking for help and giving help in the graded school became cheating.

The teacher in the one-room school showed her approval of the helping. Indeed, she often relied on it. But the graded school that made helping a sin almost worse than flunking forced the teacher to be a constant monitor and warden of the children.

Worst of all, the graded school made children suppress their natural impulse to ask and to give help.

For more than one hundred years the organization of children into grades has inhibited the behaviors necessary for children to learn as individuals. How is it that a roomful of forty children ranging in age from six to adolescence could organize so that individuals learned from each other and from the teacher, but a roomful of children of nearly the same age finds it nearly impossible to organize for learning by individuals.

The answer is in the invisible power institutions have over those inside them.

That power is strong enough to overcome teacher training, supervising standards, school architecture, administrative urging, school board policies, and the great expectations of the public.

During the 1930s educational testing demonstrated that the typical graded classroom contained children whose learning in reading and arithmetic was spread over two or more years above and two or more years below the grade being tested—a five-year range. The evidence produced a rallying cry for reform in curriculum and teaching: "Provide for individual differences!" And by the end of World War II teacher-training colleges everywhere were advising

their students to organize classrooms into small groups of three to
ten children. It was the modern way. It was the thing to do. It was
accepted practice.

Desks which had been screwed to the floor were unscrewed and
given to museums or sold at auction. New schools were furnished
with movable desks and chairs to make it easy to group children in
small groups. The goal of small-group teaching became standard
in teachers' verbalizations about "good teaching" and in supervising
manuals.

But after forty years of professional consensus on the concept of
small-group instruction, the overwhelming number of graded classrooms in the United States remain fundamentally unchanged.

- The movable furniture remains in neat rows and is rarely
  grouped differently. And the rows are designed to focus
  children's eyes on the teacher and direct their ears to her
  general lecture. Children listen in rows. Children in clus-
  ters would have to talk to each other.
- Nearly all children continue to use the same reading text,
  the same arithmetic book.
- When groupings do occur, they rarely change membership
  when shifting from reading to arithmetic.
- Record-keeping of a child's learning is by letter or number symbols that don't describe the skill learned. And the
  mark on a report card doesn't indicate what is yet to be
  learned. It is a symbol of instruction en masse rather than
  learning by individuals.

We don't intend to indict, we mean only to illustrate the power
that the institutional form has over the functions engaged in by the
people within the institution.

Teachers and administrators are all committed to individualization. But the implementation of the concept falls far short even at
the hands of those who try to break out of the institutional mold by
employing such devices as special kits of ungraded materials, classroom libraries, extra-credit projects, and special classes for the
gifted and for slow learners.

Each of the devices is a patch, and together they only hide the old institutional ways; they do not supplant them. Most educators and laymen don't seem to recognize that when minor departures from mass instruction are carried out, when some teachers in some schools do some things differently for some children some of the time, mass instruction remains for most children in most schools, most of the time.

But while most teachers mouth the institutional line about individualization, most of them do not believe that they are fulfilling the learning needs of individual children. To teachers everywhere there seem to be too many compromises and too many conditions that make learning by individuals an ideal only to be verbally honored. The teacher's soliloquy might go like this:

> I've been taught—preached at—by college professors that I should teach individuals. I have been told that in order to find out what children need academically I should give them diagnostic tests, arrange them in learning groups on the basis of the test results, and teach them a group at a time. The administration in my school agrees that we are dedicated to that approach, and all of us talk as though we do it. But do we? The standardized tests do not diagnose in reading or arithmetic. My children have grade-level scores that say they range from first-grade beginners to seventh-grade readers, but those scores don't tell me what each one needs to learn next. I have done the best I can, and there are now five different reading groups. They should have a different grade-level reader in each group, but the principal and I agree that there is no way of disguising textbooks with numbers or stars to keep the slow ones from being humiliated with a second-grade book in a fourth-grade classroom. So, I have supplementary materials from different publishers. It has taken five years of small budget appropriations and even some of my own money, but I now have a great collection. But I can't keep track of what twenty-five children are doing as they use these varied pamphlets and workbooks, and that bothers me. Therefore, while I know this is better than having all children use the same grade-level reader, I'm not really sure what's happening and how much each one is learning. I feel good about some children but sick about others. And the job of keeping four groups busy while I work with the fifth is really rough. When they sit in groups, they talk. Even when they start out whispering, the noise level grows and I have to step in. So, now I keep them busy with workbooks, even though I don't think

they do much good. But at least I can work with one small group. I wish I knew a better way.

When their innovations fail, the reformers blame uncaring and incompetent teachers and administrators. The truth is that most teachers and administrators are both caring and competent, but they are locked into roles that force them unwittingly to reject or disown the reform as surely as the body rejects the foreign heart even as the brain is crying out its thanks.

We insist (and find that some of today's students share our insight) that American education cannot be reformed until the graded and packaged school system conceived almost 150 years ago for good order rather than good education is replaced, and until teachers and administrators are once again compelled by the institutional setting to treat children as individual human beings.

Since the first primer was issued, the schools have made it their major responsibility to teach each generation how to read. And reading instruction probably has been the target of more reform than any other subject. Yet, in the 1970s, the United States of America has been forced to call for a massive "Right to Read" program because as many as 50 percent of our children are deficient in reading, and, according to a Louis Harris survey for the National Reading Council, more than 18 million Americans over the age of sixteen lack the reading ability needed to survive in today's technological society.

Educators have done far more research in reading than in any other subject taught in the school, and fifty-five years' worth of research evidence was carefully examined by Dr. Jeanne S. Chall of the Graduate School of Education, Harvard University. Her report in *Learning to Read: The Great Debate*[1] was something of a blockbuster.

Although she found a lot of educators' research to be so much rubbish, what solid evidence had been amassed pointed to an early emphasis on breaking the alphabetic code—modern phonics—as the key to learning how to read. Then why, she wondered, were most

1. Jeanne S. Chall, *Learning to Read: The Great Debate* (New York: McGraw-Hill Book Co., 1957).

schools wedded to an instructional approach that stressed meaning emphasis rather than modern phonics.

To answer her own question, Dr. Chall visited many schools across the land and talked with many teachers and administrators. She discovered that everybody she talked with was a "crusader for consensus" working in an institutional setting that demanded and rewarded consensus.

Said Dr. Chall:

> Among those concerned with beginning reading, there is a kind of schizophrenic attitude toward consensus. On the one hand, every reading specialist, no matter what his allegiance, assures us that no reading method can ever be a panacea. All talk a good deal about how important it is to recognize that different children must be allowed to learn in different ways.
>
> On the other hand, only two kinds of individualization have gained any acceptance. The first of these is differentiation in pacing: the same materials are used, the approach to teaching is unchanged, but one child moves through the material faster than another. (Differential pacing . . . is often hampered by administrative rulings and the fear that children will miss something important if accelerated.) The second kind is differentiation in content and subject matter: the child is allowed to read whatever he wants, at whatever rate he wants. But usually, only a very good teacher can make this work. Generally, only those who have already failed to learn how to read are exposed to a "no holds barred" approach as far as method is concerned.
>
> As long as this drive for consensus so strongly colors our attitude toward experimentation and change, we can expect that new methods will turn into old ones. . . .

But Dr. Chall found only a partial answer to her question. She learned that acceptance of phonics is blocked by consensus, but she wasn't sure what gave birth to, what nurtured and demanded consensus. She found many administrators who blamed the colleges that train teachers. Publishers of reading materials also were suspected as the culprits. Dr. Chall even suggested that many teachers, considering themselves to be liberal, reject modern phonics out of hand because the method is frequently advocated by people to their right on the political spectrum.

We say the overriding reason why America's public schools cannot accomplish the necessary reform in reading is the same reason why other reforms come and go. In the past, constructive change has been programmed into the schools as if they were computers that could digest, adjust, and produce the desired result. It seems not to have occurred to anyone that America's schools are mostly people—people highly conditioned by years and years of convention, pedagogy, and behavioral expectations. They operate in a system that is organized to produce and reward consensus to the rules of the system.

We have described how a social institution is organized to maintain structured behavioral patterns that override all others, making the favored ways of behaving the rewarded goals of the group. In a social institution, the participants know what to expect of each other. They live by the book of rules. If they don't, they may be punished by the institution.

What is the school system's mode and mold of behavior? You remember some of the ground rules, don't you?

> "Class, pay attention!"
> "I won't go on until we're all in our seats."
> "Everyone turn to page 45."
> "Now, by the numbers, everybody jump with your feet apart and clap your hands over your head."
> "Will everyone line up and stand quietly; otherwise, we can't go to the library today."
> "Quiet, please!"

The fact that everyone—no matter what their generation or where they make their home—can recall these ground rules expressed by America's teachers down through the years of the graded school illustrates how the social institution called the school has standardized not only behavior but even the catch phrases that organize that behavior.

Our public school system is an institution where members go through rituals handed down by tradition, where they behave according to customs decreed long ago by gods whose feet of clay have turned to dust. Truly individualized and ungraded instruction cannot possibly succeed in today's school system because the school system has been organized these many years for exactly the opposite purpose—to teach bunches of children in orderly grades.

Vernon F. Haubrich, professor in the Department of Educational Policy Studies at the University of Wisconsin, senses what we're talking about. In *Freedom, Bureaucracy, & Schooling*[2] he says:

> Teachers are part of a larger culture in which survival in school is heavily dependent upon the ability to gain acceptance within the culture of the teachers and administrators, which emphasizes certain basic outlooks and dispositions . . . The teacher has learned the system of success . . . This system of success operates inexorably to maintain a system of grading, testing, marking, sorting, and classifying which still remains intact, alive, and healthy today.

We appreciate how difficult it is to feel—let alone see—how an institution fashions and then laces tight its straitjackets. But consider these examples of mind-sets from outside the realm of education.

1. Up until the early 1900s, the rural or rich American family kept its transportation in a barn because it was an animal that made loud noises and bad smells, and because it needed protection from the elements. But for thirty years after the car had replaced the horse, the transportation was still contained in a barnlike garage separate from the house, even though the horses under the hood did not require such isolation and even though it was exceedingly inconvenient for the family to walk some distance through the foulest weather to get to and from the car.

2. It was in 1862, during the Civil War, that the ironclad ship, the *Monitor,* showed the *Merrimac* how its gun turret revolved 360 degrees. But into the early twentieth century the navy was still using the Great White Fleet of mighty battleships, which, like sailing ships whose guns were to fire broadside, were forced to turn sharply in order to aim their guns, because the turrets had a traverse of well under 45 degrees.

The teacher, walled in his Prussian box like one of a trayful of ice cubes or one of a dozen eggs in a carton, knows only that he is

2. Vernon F. Haubrich, *Freedom, Bureaucracy, and Schooling* (Washington, D.C.: Association for Supervision and Curriculum Development, 1971).

expected to be the peddler of information from one set of books for reading, one set of books for social studies, and one set of books for mathematics. Furthermore, he knows that he is expected to be the one true source of learning and the head of a classroomful of children, whose attention must be riveted on him if learning is to take place. His peers, the administration, and the teachers of teachers expect that he will behave in this way come hell or high failure.

All teachers in the institution are rewarded according to how well they follow the institution's rituals and customs. The teacher who lives up to expectations gets the approval of his peers, the "best" students, promotion, and an enviable reputation and status among parents who cannot imagine that the public school system might be organized in such a way as to harm their children. Students also are rewarded for their conformity to the behavior required by the system: high marks, promotion, smiles from teacher, a seat up front, passes when they want them, election to the honor society, and recommendations to the right college.

Critics have assumed in the past that the good teacher and effective supervisor could and would break out of the institutional mold and do what all of the reputable testing and research have shown needs to be done: develop the mental and physical well-being of each human according to his abilities and capabilities. It was further assumed that teachers and supervisors who couldn't or wouldn't were obstinate, old-fashioned, or just plain bad teachers and administrators. The fact is that teachers and administrators immersed in the graded system we have described tend to do the human thing and identify with, or personify, their condition. Thus, criticism of educators' functions are seen and are felt as personal attacks which have to be defended.

Unfortunately, much of today's criticism of education in America is most harsh toward this natural human defense.

The fact is that educators have been turned into schizophrenics. All the pedagogy lauds the virtues of individualized instruction: not one educator could be found who would defend the lock-step behavior produced by our century-old allegiance to *gut anordnung und gut wirksamkeit.* But in American public education, rhetoric is not to be confused with reality. In the Americanized Prussian school, the teacher soon learns that he must somehow live with the fact that what everybody agrees should be, is not.

If you see a wedding cake in the baker's display case and place your order for it, you can expect to receive a cake like the sample. If you order the likeness of the floor model in the car showroom, you can expect to have a facsimile delivered sometime. But if you go to your local school expecting to find the individualized learning that everyone in education says is supposed to be there, you will find much verbalization but little evidence.

All along it has been the social institution called the public school system that has compelled its members to behave according to the requirements for *efficient management* of masses of children, rather than the *effective learning* by individual children. It is our conclusion, therefore, that it is not possible to try to affect reform by just tinkering with curriculum, class size, teacher training, school organization, or the middle school instead of a junior high school.

Necessary reform can come only by radical alteration of the institution, by creation of an entirely new way of life for its members.

It is more than a century now since the grading and packaging began to bring order and efficient people management to American public education. And while the packaging was going on, there also was appending. The more each generation learned (mostly out of school), the more it had to pass on to its heirs in school. Knowledge begat knowledge and courses begat courses.

Not only was there a proliferation of courses to satisfy new intellectual requirements, but there were added on such functions as a library, physical education, the fine arts, the industrial arts/vocational education, and guidance/testing. The list of appendages today is as long as a hickory stick, maybe longer.

Now it is time to replace the appended and graded schools. The school system has to be stripped of those appended functions it has sometimes undertaken reluctantly and almost always implemented badly.

But how shall we replace this gigantic institution that took so many years to organize children and subject matter for the sake of efficiency, while at the same time it destroyed the environment that enabled children to learn naturally according to their abilities instead of according to their age and grade?

We have to start with the one-room school.

Not for a minute do we ask that urban America of the late twentieth century resurrect and reinstate the anachronistic one-room school of poverty and isolation, with limited resources, hard benches, potbellied stoves, and youngsters sewn into red flannel from fall to spring.

But the old truths about people and how they learn are not anachronisms, and never were and never will be. They were modern in Eden and they will be modern in the first Levittown on the moon. And we have learned much in addition to these truths. So, we propose to build upon that old—and new—foundation a series of institutions designed for effective learning by individuals and not for effective management of masses of children.

In the system we envision, education would not be restricted to schools, and learning would not be restricted to a population aged five to eighteen.

It is our intention that the series of new institutions shall not be for all people—but for each person and all ages. The difference is great and significant. In place of the inflexible class or grade plan for all children, for example, would be a very flexible individual program for development that would provide for and encourage learning in settings other than the school and other than even the new institutions we propose creating.

The professionals employed by the institutions would succeed and be rewarded according to how well they satisfy the needs of the individuals whom they serve, not according to how well they submit to the consensus demanded by ancient institutional traditions.

As cleanly and painlessly as possible, incisions would be made in the body fat of the supermarket school system to enable the removal of guidance/testing, physical education and health, the fine and industrial arts, the library, and vocational education.

We recognize that organs normally are not excised unless they are diseased or are performing poorly so as to endanger the health of the host. That is precisely why we recommend the radical surgery just described. The organs mentioned are not working well, and those placed in most jeopardy by their malfunction—America's children—are in need of prompt relief.

Guidance was originally appended to the schools to perform such services as helping students choose from among a growing list of elective courses, helping students match themselves to a college and career, helping students with personal problems, and helping students to acquire better study habits. But again, reality never linked up to rhetoric; performance fell far short of advance billing.

Guidance counselors are guided more by the requirements and behavior of the institution than by the theories that undergird their calling. It is far more important that they conform to the rules of the institution than that they serve students and their parents.

It is essential, therefore, that guidance counselors be placed into a new setting that encourages them to practice the theories and regard students and their parents—and other residents of the community who might use their services—as clients. Removed from the present school, guidance counselors, psychologists, and others would work together to diagnose individual needs for mental and physical development, to prescribe the best individual program to meet those needs, and to evaluate learning. And the learning to be evaluated would be what individuals have learned in school *and* learned outside of school. The focus would be on the client, not on the place called school and not on education-labeled school curricula.

But our new institutions for guidance and evaluation also would be concerned with the work of the other new educational institutions to determine how well they are doing the job they are designed to do, how well programs designed for students are working for students.

All of the other excisions would be accomplished with the same goal in mind—to remove functions from an institution whose form has not permitted them to fulfill their promise and to place them into settings that impel the promise to be fulfilled.

It is paradoxical, but if such functions as guidance and such life essentials as art and music are ever to get closer to children, they must be taken out of today's schools.

The school's programs for the physical development and health of children have resulted in institutional forms called physical education, sports, and health education. But the roles of the physical education teachers, coaches, doctors, nurses, and dentists are unrelated to each other and are of little benefit to the child and his family. The institutional forms controlling these professionally competent people have prevented them from functioning effectively.

Physical education mostly has meant playing different games each season where the ball changes size and shape, but with no measure of results for individual children. Educators and laymen alike have lived with the old Roman error that if one saw it in the Coliseum—the high school gym or football stadium—it had to be good for everybody in the Empire.

Doctors and nurses have been relegated to costly but perfunctory inspections and Band-Aid care.

A generation ago, the school made the arts into watercolor posters and installed them as subjects to be taught occasionally in the elementary school and only as electives in the high school. And good art teachers have struggled against the handicaps. We would restore the arts to the people by creating a community center where people of all ages could practice the arts and crafts day and night—in as many different ways as their talents and interests can conceive. Combined with the arts center would be a community museum and library. Today's school calls the library a resource center, but still this appended function is very often underused and undermarketed. Students have limited access, adults none, and it closes early every day and all day on Saturday and Sunday. We would make the library available to the whole community day and night and on Saturday and Sunday.

The stigma of vocational education would be erased by a new institution and series of programs devoted to helping all young people aged fourteen to eighteen plan careers and engage in work experiences—apprenticed to an airplane mechanic or a zoologist, and to persons in nearly every occupation in between. Our young people have been closed out of the legitimate activities of the adult world. Yet they crave the reality as well as the symbols of maturity.

We also propose that youths engage in service to the social issues and needs of the times. Let them learn the toughness of solving people's problems firsthand as aides to family agencies, social workers, and other voluntary health and welfare institutions. Enthusiasm is a hallmark of youth. Emotional vigor and physical strength are their inheritance. Let us provide real work experiences for our millions of adolescents so that they might give of themselves while they learn.

The school, stripped of its appendages, would be concerned with the mental and social development of the individual. It would be free to use old and new forms, materials, and techniques that cater to the individual's intellectual and social needs in varied settings designed for students and not to satisfy *gut anordnung und gut wirksamkeit.* Mass handling has become mishandling.

For years the teacher has pleaded for the right environment and enough time to teach. We plan to give the student the right environments and enough time to learn, from teachers who are made of flesh and blood—and paper and cellulose acetate and electronic impulses and tubes. Accordingly, in later chapters we have described a wide variety of settings and methods for learning. Some are new, some are old, and some are being tried even now. All of them—and more—need to be critically tested as the people grow in their understanding that education is a process that takes many forms in many different settings.

This combination of new institutions, that once more would impel learning by individuals instead of instruction for the masses, is our Design for Community Education. And that is what this book is all about.

The United States of America in the last two decades has poured billions into the public schools through the National Defense

Education Act, the Vocational Education Acts, the monumental Elementary and Secondary Education Act, and a passel of other federal laws. The results are not impressive. Sometimes they are not even measurable.

Our series of new institutions, therefore, are not a pipe dream to be talked to death in pedagogues' seminars. They are a plan of action—a plan for learning. They plead for immediate attention from the lay public and those professional educators who can free themselves from the institutional blinders, free themselves from guilt, free themselves from the marionette strings manipulated by the institution that prevents them from their fulfillment and effectiveness.

We hope we have succeeded in describing a process by which education will become the mortar in a society that is being pulled apart. Our Education Assembly—the vital substitute for the school board—is an institution that would compel an examination of alternatives to learning and would make decisions to be publicly tested. Facts do not remove disagreement and argument, but they can reduce the temperatures of our controversies.

Education should be a source of joy instead of one more burning issue.

Two

An Assembly Rises on
the School Board's Grave

BOARDS OF EDUCATION were once considered prestigious, nonpolitical public bodies run by benign individuals of status—the "best" people in the community. But no more. In only a few wealthy suburbs is that image maintained. Frequently, even there, it is under challenge, for the rise of discontent with this venerable political form is everywhere.

Listen to the challenges!

- A young executive commuting to the city speaks: "The board had a hearing last week on next year's proposed operating budget. About $50,000 was in there for foreign language instruction in the lower grades. The board's been upping that appropriation ever since foreign languages for the elementary schools got started in one school three years ago. Well, some of us did a little research this year. We came up with some data that the program isn't all that it's cracked up to be. We really made a pretty strong case. But we were amazed at what happened. The board and the superintendent made a lame defense; they couldn't even produce evidence to indicate that the instruction gets results. Imagine! $50,000 and they didn't know what they were getting for the money!"
- A PTA president from a medium-sized district in the West

says: "I try to attend public board meetings regularly, but frankly, I don't know whether I can take many more of them. The other night the board spent two hours arguing over incidental furnishings and decor for the new school. I can't remember the last time the board took that much time to debate new curriculum. I'll be glad when my youngest graduates."

● A board member from a large county system in the South says: "Every spring the superintendent presents the board with a list of teachers whose contracts should be renewed and a list of those whose contracts should not be renewed. With over 5,000 teachers in the district, our knowledge of individuals is very limited and then it's based upon hearsay and secondhand information. We shouldn't be doing such things, but some of us, I suspect, like the sense of power."

● A black man talks about his hometown, a mid-western city approaching a population of 60,000: "We have a seven-member board of education, six white and one black, all elected at large. With 20 percent of the town and 35 percent of the children in the schools black, we don't feel we are properly represented in the establishment. They picked the one black man and the word went out to all the PTA's that he should win. Man, that's not representation; that's charity."

● A sixty-five-year-old resident of suburbia says: "Do you know what the 1970 census shows? One of every ten persons in these towns and villages is over sixty-five. Do you know what people my age are saying? We can't go on living here on retired pay. But the way they raise taxes, the school board doesn't know it. You can't find a school board member over sixty-five for miles around here."

These vignettes only hint at the fuller roll call of current criticisms expressed by frustrated Americans:

Boards miss the big picture. They are overinvolved in selecting paint colors for classrooms, hiring janitors, and selecting boiler insurance. They are rubber stamps for the superintendent. They don't know what is going on. They never heard of day care. Why can't they stand up to the teachers' organizations? When are they going to hear the students' cries for more relevant learning? What are their qualifications? Who arranges their nomination? When are they going to demonstrate they have a business sense of how to control expenditures? They care more about a winning basketball team than improving reading. They don't know what's going on. They were not really involved in the new county master plan. All decisions are made in a hurry. They try to run the schools by jumping from one crisis to another.

How did our boards of education—respected for the more than one hundred years before the last twenty—become the targets of today's criticisms? The conventional rhetoric that describes what boards should be doesn't help us understand what went wrong. Typical of the language that tells a school board member what his role is supposed to be is that contained in two documents published by the New Jersey School Boards Association:

> The school board should operate as a policy-making body, basing its policies on the best educational advice available, and properly delegating the execution of these policies to its professional administrator and staff.
>
> The most important functions of a school board are the formulation of policies and the judgment of results. The board makes policies to provide a broad guide for action by school personnel so that schools may operate efficiently. Board members should recognize that their responsibility is not to run the schools, but to see that the schools are well run.
>
> Written policies provide for delegation of authority, thus maintaining control and reducing the need for board discussion on minor matters.

The board that runs the schools should represent the people of the district—all of them. It should be both a follower and a leader of constructive public opinion. It should be a policy-making body, translating the people's best hopes and wisest intents for the education of their young into priority goals, guidelines, directives, and controls that give direction to the professional educators in the board's employ. The board that runs the schools should use its best judgment and tax according to the people's ability to pay for the fulfillment of their best hopes and wisest intents. Finally, it should hold the professional educators charged with implementing policies responsible for those decisions and programs that are of their making.

That's what the board that runs the schools should be. It is not.

Today's board is not representative, not an effective legislative body, not able to hold educators accountable for their programs' performance. It is the wrong institution in the wrong time and place.

To know why the school board of the latter third of the twentieth century is not right for the times, it is necessary once again to look backward to the time for which it was right. Our forefathers conceived of the one-room school to expose their young to the rudiments necessary for literacy. To oversee this simple institution, our ancestors created another simple institution—a small committee of men to represent the common will, whose responsibilities were to see to the erection and maintenance of the building, to hire a teacher, to establish the curriculum, and, finally, to raise the public funds necessary to accomplish all of the foregoing.

The committee was both a legislative and an executive body. As a committee, the school trustees performed their several duties quite effectively, because the committee and its functions were well-suited to each other in that time and place.

But the small committee of trustees no longer works. Because the simple institution that was the one-room school is now a system of a dozen, fifty, one hundred, or several hundred schools—all with many rooms. The teachers now number more than one—frequently more than a thousand and one—and they are supervised by department chairmen, assistant principals, principals, directors, supervisors, specialists, assistant superintendents, and superintendents. Furthermore, education today is more than readin', 'ritin, and 'rithmetic. It is a complex undertaking for great numbers of children.

Consider what has happened to the board's ability to represent the people. In a younger America, the committee of trustees represented perhaps fifty to one hundred families, all of whom were conceived in the same ethnic and social womb. The represented and the representatives were neighbors. It was almost impossible for the trustees to harbor ideas about schooling that were not shared by their familiar constituency.

Today's school board is that same rural committee of trustees; only the names have been changed. But now the trustees are supposed to represent thousands—sometimes hundreds of thousands—of families who are increasingly polyphyletic and nomadic. It is very bad representation. Important legislation can be—and frequently is—enacted by trustees without either the knowledge or consent of a constituency they only remotely know or understand.

The perpetuation of the colonial committee as a modern board of education has made it impossible for the trustees to be representative of the population they serve—whether the board be elected or appointed, whether it be in the city or the suburbs.

The colonial committee could combine the two major duties needed to provide a limited education to the children of sparsely settled rural areas. The school committee was the local lawmaker for education. It was its own principal, supervisor, and administrative agency.

But in the last 150 years a vast complex of schools and functions and a superstructure for administration have developed while the governing body has remained essentially unchanged. It remains what it was—a committee. Accordingly, its members are held fast by its form. They continue to behave, to operate as that social organization and its heritage impels them.

So, we see doctors, engineers, housewives, business leaders, the college graduate, and the eighth-grade graduate, transformed by the invisible constraints and pressures of this institutional form into school board members. They read from an invisible script, unaware of how rigidly they are held to the lines of a play written long before their term of office began. Why is this so?

We all react with instinctive dislike to the idea that we are not masters of our own behavior. And a new board of education member is no exception. He frequently arrives with secret or open resolves to speak his own mind, to be his own man, to follow his own conscience, to get the facts, to work for the best interests of the children, to guard the tax dollar. And most members leave the board years later believing that by and large they have abided by their early goals and standards.

Yet, to the outside observer in increasing numbers, this comforting self-appraisal is a form of self-deception. For, in fact, the committee size and structure of the board of education inhibits these behaviors while seeming to permit them. A committee of part-time laymen—not equipped with an investigating staff of its own, not organized to hold hearings and to listen to expert testimony, not equipped with the skills for drawing up legislative requirements, unable to ask for evaluative reports (or to review them if received), limited in its abilities to keep fiscal expenditures related to purposes —is a social organism with a body poorly built for its functions. One thinks of Darwin's species that did not adapt.

The lovely rhetoric which describes the task of the board of education, and from which the individual member draws his image of his equally important functions, remains words not to be confused with reality. Reality consists of agendas overwhelmingly cluttered with details of administration. That is, the board is still involved in the twentieth century version of providing the chopped wood for the pot bellied stove and hiring the one teacher: choosing uniforms for the band, determining the amount of meat needed for cafeteria sandwiches, granting permissions to attend conferences, awarding contracts for supplies, reviewing specifications to construct playing fields, hiring custodians, composing a letter to the police commissioner requesting a crossing guard at a street intersection, questioning the resignations of several teachers, listening to a recommendation that a course in sociology be added to the high school curriculum—asking for costs but accepting the response that since no additional staff will be required no significant cost is anticipated.

These are a random sample of conventional and universal items that fill the meetings of rural, suburban, and urban boards of education. Frequently these items are introduced by members of the board who chair a committee under whose jurisdiction the agenda item falls. The procedure helps the board's appearance of having probed the background of the topic, when in reality this seldom occurs.

A further consequence of the board's preoccupation with internal operation of the schools is to place blinders and cataracts on their vision. They see narrowly and think small. They may add or subtract a grade to a junior high school and call it a middle school, but they seem incapable of thinking about whole new forms.

It is significant that the books on how boards of education should operate admonish members against becoming bogged down in the trivia of administration. Similarly, the courses designed to prepare school administrators for their roles urge them to guard the prerogatives of the chief executive against the acknowledged omnipresent hazard of board encroachment. But no one questions why, given the human diversity of members of boards of education and the extraordinary differences between districts, everyone continues to believe that the remedy lies in preachment, admonition, and training instead of in changing the form that makes puppets of the people. The form of a social institution can shape the behavior of the institution's members contrary to the language used to describe the institution's purposes and its members' intentions. It seems clear to us that if public policy governing education is to be changed, the tasks performed by those chosen or elected to represent the public will must be changed. And this requires the fashioning of a new public body to govern education.

The current effort in some of our major cities toward that goal is called decentralization. Critics agree that the central bureaucracies of the large cities have tended to stultify educational reforms, made responsibility difficult to focus, added to costs, and become unresponsive to parents and children.

The popular hope, or presumption, is that decentralization in the big cities will help restore the close ties between the represented and their representatives. So, in New York City and Detroit, the central board of education has given up some of its authority to community boards. But we can find scant evidence to justify optimism that this latest attempt to make the eighteenh century committee work in the late twentieth century will succeed.

Only the week after the 1970 election of the thirty or so New York City community boards, *The New York Times* reported on their unrepresentativeness: "An analysis of last week's local school board elections made by the United Parents' Associations has shown that many communities elected local boards that did not reflect the ethnic composition of the public-school population.

"In some districts with sizeable numbers of black and Puerto Rican pupils, few, if any, blacks or Puerto Ricans were elected to the local boards."

Decentralization came to Detroit in 1971. The old seven-member board of education was replaced by a new thirteen-member central board and eight five-member regional boards. It was all done in the name of better representation—community control, power to the people. But this is what Wiliam Grant reported in the *Christian Science Monitor* in February 1971: "There are only 13 blacks among the 45 regional and central board members, and only three on the central board. Only two of the eight regions have black-controlled boards, although five of the regions have a majority of black students. Citywide, the school system is 65 percent black."

The steady decline in the American school board's capability to be representative was recorded by Kenneth H. Hansen in 1963: "The number of boards is steadily decreasing as districts are consolidated, but very small districts quite frequently have as large school boards as do much more populous districts. Thus, in 1961, 91 percent of the school boards in the United States had jurisdiction over less than 20 percent of the school children of the nation."

A seven-member board governs the schools of Los Angeles, a city of almost 2.8 million persons, and a seven-member board also governs the one school in Rochelle Park, New Jersey—population 6,400. Back across the country in San Diego, just five trustees represent nearly 700,000 persons and head a school system of approximately 120,000 students.

In a 1967 study of almost 500 school districts, the Educational

Research Service reported that 96 percent of districts with an enrollment of 12,000 to 24,999 were governed by a board of education with nine or fewer members. But *83 percent* of the districts with an enrollment in excess of 100,000 *also* were governed by a board of nine members or less.

But the unrepresentative colonial committee masking as a modern board of education doesn't exist only in the big city, and blacks and Puerto Ricans are not the only ones who often find themselves without representation and a voice inside the school system. The unrepresented are everywhere.

At a 1969 seminar sponsored by the National School Boards Association, Roald F. Campbell, then dean of the Graduate School of Education at the University of Chicago, warned that school boards in larger districts would have to accommodate themselves to the future.

"The board of education itself will tend to become a more representative body," he said.

> The elitist concept of the board, and one with which many of us have been comfortable, is being challenged on many fronts. Increasing representativeness of boards will probably come whether board members are appointed or elected. In those districts where the appointment procedure is employed, if appointment does not provide board members from many segments of the community, the procedure will probably be changed by the state legislature.
>
> Even if appointing officials are committed to a representative board, the achievement of such a goal is not entirely possible. There are, for instance, more ethnic groups and more regional areas in most cities than can ever be accommodated on most boards with seven to eleven members. Nor will all of these problems be resolved by the election of board members. If elections be at large, some groups will again be left out. This will probably lead to the establishment of areas . . . from which school board members are to be elected.

Dr. Campbell saw the need and the inevitability of greater representation on school boards, but he seemed uncertain how this could be achieved given the size of today's boards of education.

Decentralization might help, but it simply multiplies the old board of education. Society has a mind-set that the size of school boards was for all time established as a number between five and twelve. It is as though society were trapped into accepting the problem with built-in absolutes it couldn't change. The old trick of connecting nine dots on a sheet of paper with just three straight lines is insoluble if our minds accept the assumption that the lines cannot extend out onto the paper beyond the dots. Once that assumption is disposed of, with the recognition that it is self-imposed, the solution to the problem is evident. If we discard the self-imposed assumption that to get greater representation we need to repeat the pattern of the small, colonial school committee, the direction toward the answer becomes clear. The answer is to form a new body of greater size, to establish voting districts for education across the face of a city or school district, and to send representatives to the new governing body.

We call this new body an Education Assembly. It would be large, but it would not be elected at large. And its size would serve to promote its performance as a legislative body, while tending to reduce the propensity to become its own executive agent again.

The new body would be designed to perform better four major tasks necessary to improve education. First, it would provide for greater representation. Second, the assembly would be internally organized to function as a legislative body with the necessary structure and staff to perform that role efficiently. Third, the assembly would hold the executive agency accountable for the effectiveness with which programs are carried out. And fourth, the assembly, freed from administrative chores and operational responsibilities, would be able to examine alternative ways of reaching educational objectives in addition to or instead of present school forms.

To determine optimum size for a representative body with legislative functions is an empirical process for which some historical guidelines exist. The whole population to be served is a factor. A legislature of 500 to serve a population of 1,000 would be absurd. Yet the Athenians had an assembly of 1,500 which legislated without constitutional restraints for a citizenry of some 40,000 and a total population of a quarter million, including slaves and the free foreign born. Members lost their identity in the mass and Athens lost its freedom. Accordingly, an assembly with many hundreds of members is considered too cumbersome a body for our purposes. On the other hand, there is the need for a body not so small as to preclude the internal organization needed for legislative effectiveness. We already have seen that 12 or less people become a committee. A committee can serve a larger body as its agent for a designated purpose but it does not operate well as an independent deliberative group. At what number, between 5 and 500 do we choose to organize the Education Assembly? The answer is that no one size will do everywhere. For communities of different size, different population characteristics, and different residential patterns there would need to be Education Assemblies of different sizes.

Large metropolitan districts ranging up to 500,000 in population could choose to have Education Assemblies ranging from 50 to near 200 members. Each community would analyze present residential patterns, neighborhood identities, ethnic distribution—the human ecology of the city—and commercial centers, industrial areas, and transportation networks to map the areas with which residents feel some natural identity in order to set election districts.

Districts established according to the several criteria suggested will scarcely be of the same population size. Therefore, the number of representatives from districts may vary. Or single representatives may carry a weighted vote proportional to their district's population. Further, given a single body legislature the need may be recognized for stabilizing discussion through the appointment by the assembly of "elder statesmen" from among the community's leaders. And the need for special representation from young people below eighteen years of age may persuade many assemblies to include a sizeable number of representatives elected from that age group rather than from a geographic district. The same election procedure might be applied to elect people over sixty-five. The goal is a broadly based representative body. The means would be varied.

The Education Assembly would be organized into standing and ad hoc committees which would conduct hearings to determine the community's needs; take expert testimony; publish staff reports detailing alternative ways of reaching an educational goal; analyze the merits, demerits, and costs of each of the alternatives; and convert best judgment into appropriate legislation.

As standard procedure, all legislation establishing new programs would require a preliminary evaluation of the new programs within ninety days of inauguration, and an annual audit. The assembly would establish a program evaluation agency to serve it for this purpose. In areas of major change, where an additional review is desired, the Education Assembly should contract for intensive appraisal and audit by an outside agency. All reviews and reports upon completion would be made public.

The Education Assembly would establish a governing board for each agency and institution it authorizes. These local boards would be elected by residents of the area and by the people served. The board would be the local community's representatives holding agencies accountable for the roles set by the assembly's legislation and keeping them close to the people served.

The Education Assembly would work with other agencies of government. One of the weaknesses of our present processes is the isolation of the schools and their boards of education from the other operations of local government. This isolation was engendered and maintained because of the fear that politics and the schools would mix at the cost of good education. Unfortunately, the price paid for immunity to political patronage and party pressures has been fragmented health programs and limited resources being wasted on duplicate and overlapping programs. School playing fields unrelated to and unused by municipal recreation activities, plans for mass housing units that ignore educational needs, and highways and other transportation routes changed without reference to the plans of boards of education have been unhappy commonplaces.

There are towns, communities, and neighborhoods where planning for education is considered too important to involve the local board of education. There is scarcely a municipality where the neglect of educational needs while preparing the master plan isn't due in large measure to the traditional aloofness displayed by boards of education toward other branches of government.

Our Education Assembly would be involved.

Involved because education receives most of the local tax revenue and is a major user of land, and because those who are responsible for educational planning must be vitally concerned with health services, recreation, transportation, the arts, museums, libraries, theaters, and the general life of the community.

The Education Assembly would move from the fiction of non-involvement to the reality of direct cooperation with other agencies in planning total service to the community. And the Education Assembly as a new legislative arm of state government would have the power to tax and borrow money for the purposes of education.

It is hoped that many of the restraints now imposed on boards of education by state governments, such as those limiting tax rates and requiring more than a simple majority to pass a referendum, would be relaxed, because these restrictions are historically related to education's political isolation and the need to restrain local boards of education.

Because institutional form tends to control institutional functions, we strongly advocate the abolition of school committees and boards of education that are anachronistic forms in twentieth century urban America.

In their place we urge a new legislative body that is . . .

- broadly representative.
- organized to determine the desires and needs of a community for better education.
- free of the old assumption that schools are the only places where learning can take place.
- free of the old assumption that children are education's only clients.
- free of the old assumption that the concerns of other governmental agencies are not also its concerns.
- required by design to hold administrators accountable. No longer would a board of education turn to its executive arm for an accounting only to say in bewilderment, "We have met the administrator, and he is us."

- required by design to measure and evaluate the performance of each agency it creates.

This new legislative body—the Education Assembly—is the first of our new forms for education. It is long overdue for American education.

Three

Guidance Leaves School to
Serve Its Clients

PARENTS IN AMERICA look to their child's teacher or guidance counselor for an accounting of what is happening to their child.

But the teacher and the guidance counselor cannot give a good account. They are members of an institution that has developed subtle—frequently invisible—rules designed for its own perpetuation and enhancement. There are rewards, punishments, and internal adjustments designed to mold and control the behavior of all its members. Guidance personnel are caught fast in a web of relationships which inhibit and deny their ability to function. The fault, once again, will not be found in the rhetoric describing the function guidance is supposed to perform.

The guidance function in the school is intended by the textbooks on the subject:

1. to assist parents in understanding the consequences of the school's efforts in behalf of their child;
2. to assist parents in understanding the factors that influence their child's learning;
3. to recommend to parents, child, and teachers those changes that would upgrade learning;
4. to assist child and parents to make educational and vocational decisions;
5. to provide personal counseling for the child.

43

But in the city tenement, in the suburban split level, and in the rural farmhouse there are many parents who are concerned about what is happening to their children in school. And usually the alarm is aggravated by severe frustration at their inability to find out why it is happening.

Because the institution has impressed upon the public that the system does not fail—only students do—the parents first turn to their children for answers. And the questions are heavily laced with implied blame.

"Shouldn't you have more homework to do? Wouldn't that help?"

"Is it that you simply don't understand what the teacher says? Why don't you ask for extra help!"

"Are you busy talking or fooling around when you should be paying attention?"

"Don't you realize how important algebra is? It trains the mind; everybody knows that."

"Are you scared when you take a test? Don't be; the score doesn't matter that much."

"Why an F? Don't you ever want to get anywhere?"

The child's answers (if he gives any) usually tell the parents nothing that satisfies them, although they may imply much.

"I get my homework done in school."

"Staying after school won't help."

"Sure, I pay attention. Sometimes, though, I lose track of what the teacher is talking about."

"Algebra is dumb. Who needs it?"

"No, I don't get scared over a test. But what do you mean the score doesn't matter? Where do you think my grade comes from?"

After a prolonged but fruitless exchange of such questions and answers has led at least to an epidemic of Excedrin headaches and at worst to increased estrangement between the generations, the parents may turn to the school for answers and help. Whether they do or not is dependent mostly on their social and economic class. The middle class will sometimes turn to the school for help. The working class, the poor, and the nonwhite almost never come on their own initiative.

A phone call or visit to the school office produces the following information: the child's teacher can be seen on Tuesday afternoon between 3 and 4 P.M. by making an appointment at least two days in advance. A meeting can be arranged with the guidance counselor almost any day at midmorning or early afternoon, but an appointment must be made at least the day before.

The majority of working fathers cannot meet any of the suggested appointments. And nearly one out of every two married women work. Because some nonworking mothers feel uncomfortable and inadequate coping with the school alone, they also do not go to see the teacher and/or counselor.

So, these initial responses by the school prevent many parents from going any further in their search for answers to what is happening to their child in school.

For those parents able and willing to make an appointment at the convenience of their child's teacher or counselor, the result may not be worth the effort. The teacher, because the institution compels him to be suspicious of the parent's questioning of the institution and its members, is on the defensive, nervous. The parent, who at home may have talked herself into being a strong and effective advocate for her child, suddenly finds herself acting sheepishly and offering apologies for disturbing the teacher. With both parties on the defensive and jittery, the meeting is apt to dissolve quickly without being productive.

Here is how the script might read for the teacher dealing with the unwelcome outsider:

> Your child should be doing better; he's smart enough. I think his trouble is that he isn't trying hard. He appears to be disinterested; I've caught him daydreaming from time to time. If he does need extra help, I am ready to give it. I stay after school until 4 P.M. every Wednesday afternoon to give extra help to those children who ask for it. But they have to ask my help; I won't go to them. *They* have to be motivated. Don't you agree?

After the nervousness of meeting the teacher has worn off like a needleful of Novocaine after the dentist's visit, the parent discovers the hurt hasn't gone away—the hurt that a parent feels when something is happening to her child and she can't do anything about it.

She asked why it's happening, but all that she learned is that her child "isn't trying hard—doesn't care."

"But why doesn't he care?" is the question she still asks. Nobody hears it and nobody answers it.

For some parents, of course, the teacher's statements simply reinforce their suspicion that their child is lazy and foolish and doesn't care about what he's doing to them or to himself. They begin the next round of questions and answers with their child, the questions framed even more like accusations and the answers sounding even more unresponsive and perhaps even surly.

The interview with the guidance counselor is not likely to go much better. The institution compels the typical counselor to be an apologist for the school in order to maintain his favorable status with teachers and the institution.

"According to his records," says the counselor,

> your child has potential. I would suggest that in subjects where he's not doing well, or in which he has the least interest, he should try that much harder—study more. I don't know whether you are aware of it, but I just had your child in here last semester to discuss his grades. I reminded him then that if he wants to go to college or get a good job, he'll have to do better.

Why have these middle-class parents received platitudes instead of answers? Why have teachers and counselors been forced into defensive postures rather than required to provide help?

We assert that the institution is to blame for the way guidance counselors behave, that the institution has shaped the teachers' attitudes toward children and their parents.

Unfortunately, schools substitute high rhetoric for results. Words describing purposes are blindly accepted as evidence of performance, while institutional relationships dictate practices that are very contrary to those purposes. Schools are not unique in this; they are just exceptionally good at it.

Teachers learn to accept the confounding dichotomy of rhetoric versus reality as part of the process of learning how to live in the school as an institution. For example, teachers are taught that they should be understanding of children's needs, they should know the very wide range of differences among children of the same age. Teachers should know how children learn, the conditions that facilitate learning, the factors that limit children's performance, and what they should do about them. They should know how to arouse children's interests and motivate learning.

But the social organism called the school is a group of teachers who learn a very different set of things to believe about children. From the institution they learn that children are reluctant learners sometimes capable of frustrating the teacher's work. And from this viewpoint derives the institutional description of the number of children in a class as the "teacher's load." Children are a barge to be towed and a bale to be lifted.

Because teaching is thought of as a burden, the fault when learning is poor or not achieved is determined by the institution to lie with the student—the reluctant learner. The teacher has done well; the student has done poorly. When reasons for the student's failure are sought, the institution goes looking in a world that is not of the teacher's making—the home and the community environment. It might be in the inner city:

- "He lives with his grandmother because his parents are separated."
- "He's sickly; he can't be getting the right diet."
- "He's always falling asleep in class; how lazy can a person be."
- "He's been absent over forty times this year."
- "I don't know where his mind could be."
- "I had his older brother; none of that family are interested in school."
- "What a neighborhood! I don't know how those people can live like that."

Or it might be in suburbia that the institution goes looking:

- "I hear her father just lost his job because of drinking."
- "That's not her real mother; both parents have been married two or three times."

- "The mother is one of those pushy types. You know, ballet lessons on Tuesday, orthodontist on Wednesday, Girl Scouts on Thursday, church group, tutoring in Latin, and all that sort of thing."
- "Her mother will blame you for every test her precious fails."
- "She runs wild; I think she's on drugs."
- "That whole crowd is turned off."

One can accept with reservations the assumption behind each of these statements that they represent factors that inhibit learning. But nowhere in our teacher's litany of the woes that afflict children is there any implication that the school or the teachers have a compensatory role. In fact, each statement is made with a finality that implies that no action will be taken—or that action is in fact impossible in view of the circumstances.

If one were to assume that the school, having discovered that a child is without a father, would place the child with male teachers and provide activities designed to give masculine support, one would assume too much. If one assumed that, given a case of chronic fatigue in a youngster, the school would determine that the child is not lazy but needs help, one would assume too much.

We are dealing here with more than the common occurrence of saying one thing and doing another. Teachers are no more hypocritical than the rest of mankind, and in terms of their devotion to children, they probably are less hypocritical than the rest of us.

But the institution has created a climate for schizophrenics. Teachers repeat the rhetoric of high purpose, but they complain to each other about the reasons the high purposes cannot be accomplished. And they believe themselves in each case. They see no difference between the two verbalizations. However, most of them end up behaving in harmony with the language of the institution— the language that can only find fault outside the institution.

Exceptional teachers, like exceptional people in every walk of life, can and do overcome the system. But their very uniqueness illustrates the power the institution has over all of the other teachers to conform to its standards. The effects of such power are what is revealed in the private conversations of teachers.

Unfortunately, guidance personnel are compelled to be just as schizophrenic. The role of the guidance counselor began to emerge just after World War II as a mutation from the deans of boys and girls in the larger districts whose primary function it was to get students into the college of their choice.

Guidance and counseling were given a new emphasis just after Sputnik went into orbit and Americans went into shock (1957). The National Defense Education Act that followed in Sputnik's vapor trail opened the federal treasury to colleges wishing to train counselors and to school districts wanting to employ them. Most colleges and school districts did.

In the beginning counselors were employed only in junior and senior high schools, and still mostly for the purpose of placing students in college. Now there is an increasing number of counselors in the elementary schools. And the counselor's role has so broadened that in theory at least the counselor is now the one person in the school who is most responsive to all of the child's needs and wants and his parents' hopes and fears, and most responsible for guiding the child successfully through twelve years of public schooling and into the college or job best suited for him.

That is the theory. The practice is something else. A high school principal being interviewed by a newspaper writer helped put the finger on why the counselor has difficulty fulfilling the role as outlined in the textbooks, described by college professors, and defined in school manuals.

There is a great deal of latent animosity between teachers and counselors, the principal said. He went on to categorize the complaints most often made against counselors by teachers.

- "Guidance counselors are too overprotective of students. They're soft touches—when the teacher feels the kid isn't worth saving anyway.
- "Guidance counselors are too eager to please parents and/ or students.

● "The teacher sometimes sees the counselor as a threat to
his own position."

Then, in reference to another teacher complaint, the principal
said, "A teacher who complains that the counselor steers students
away from his class is probably putting the blame in the wrong
place."

What the principal was not asked by the interviewer, and thus
did not answer, are the questions, Why do teachers react in this
manner? Are most counselors able to overcome the pressure that
the complaints of their colleagues force upon them?

The answer to both questions lies in the way the institution con-
ceives the counselor's role, rather than the way it is conceived by
the theorists, the policy manual, and even the counselor himself.

The counselor is employed as a member of the faculty; in fact,
it is probable that he once was a teacher in the same system. The
institution says that his role is one of supporting teachers. There
is a double meaning to the word "support." The counselor is to
support the teacher in the sense that he is expected to assist and
back up the teacher in her service to students.

But the counselor also is expected to support the teacher as
Stephen Decatur supported America: "Our country! In her inter-
course with foreign nations may she always be in the right; but our
country, right or wrong." The counselor is forced by the peer pressure built into the institution to offer his pledge: "Our teachers!
In their dealings with students may they always be right; but our
teachers, right or wrong."

It's a pledge that the counselor reneges on only at his own peril.
And the perils could run the gamut from angry stares in the faculty
lounge to reassignment and a more or less permanent ostracism by
fellow teachers.

As the high school principal correctly observed, the teacher is
particularly suspicious of the student when he says he has an appointment in the counselor's office. She is afraid the student will
report to the counselor either real or imagined inadequacies and
idiosyncrasies evidenced by the teacher.

Like the school board member, the counselor is forced into schizophrenia. The rhetoric of his training has prepared him to perform functions that now are in disharmony with the behavior compelled by the institution. And so it is the rare counselor indeed who is able to overcome the rules of the institution and serve the needs of students when they are in conflict with the interests of the system and of any member of the team he is pledged to support at any cost. He must be supercommitted to the role described in the textbooks or risk being denounced.

Imagine if you will a student sitting face to face with the counselor at his desk in early November. The student—a girl and a sophomore—is in tears. She has just told the counselor how miserable she is in an English class where the teacher divides class time between shouting for order in the room and reviewing plays and movies he's seen and books he has read. "If I try to read a book or play I've borrowed from the library or brought from home," she laments, "he insists that I put it away and pay attention. But he's a bore."

The counselor is sympathetic; he knows the teacher and has heard students complain about him before. Once, two years ago, he worked very hard to get a student transferred out of the teacher's class. The teacher became incensed and told other teachers that the counselor wouldn't know a bad student if he fell over one and, furthermore, would take the word of a bad student over the word of a teacher just trying to do his job. It was unpleasant for the counselor during most of that year.

Again, he must decide whether to risk good standing among his peers (including the principal) or tell the girl she'll have to stick it out in the assigned English class. This time he prefers not to take the risk.

Of course, in most districts the institution makes it easy for the counselor to avoid having to make such painful decisions in the first place. To insure that the interests of the system and the feelings of the teachers are not jeopardized, the institution decrees that students may not transfer after the first two or three weeks of the school year. And to make extra sure that students don't get the upper hand, the school system might rule that transfers can be affected only at the suggestion of the teacher who is losing the student and with the approval of the teacher who must accept the student.

Changes made solely for the sake of improving learning by individual children are seen as disruptive, a breaking of those most sacred rules that require the institution to operate smoothly for its adult participants even at the cost of denying services to its student members.

The books and professors that train guidance counselors tell them to administer and interpret the results of standardized tests for the benefit of the students they serve. But again, institutional behavior gets in the way of the good intent.

The truth is that a student's performance on a standardized test often is not used to promote his learning, and sometimes it is misused so that the student's learning is impeded. And not infrequently, the student will complete most of his twelve years in public schools without he or his parents even knowing the results of all the years of testing, let alone what the results mean and how they have been used, unused, or misused.

Standardized tests that measure student achievement in major subject areas traditionally are given to all students in all grades every year, or in alternate years. Learning ability tests that measure aptitude and intelligence customarily are administered to all students two to four times during their twelve-year enrollment. And the student contemplating college likely will take another learning ability test (a college entrance examination) in his junior or senior year, or both.

The institution requires the testing, but it requires no hard evidence that the consequences of the testing have substantially affected the learning of individual students. In fact, the guidance counselor and the teacher soon discover that the written and unwritten rules that dictate institutional behavior simply do not encourage the counselor or the teacher to make test results work for students.

When the results of achievement and learning ability tests *are* used, they may serve only as support for institutional decisions that label a student slow, average, or above average.

When the labels have been affixed, students may be assigned within their grade (or subjects) to classes composed only of slow students, or average students, or above average students.

Minority groups have charged that test results used to justify teaching have resulted in racially segregated classes, because the tests were technically poor and the schools were biased. They have been correct about the tests being poor instruments for assigning students to fast, slow, and average classes.

In a speech in the spring of 1971, Henry S. Dyer, vice-president of the Educational Testing Service, said "it is abundantly clear that most consumers of achievement test results (counselors and teachers) seem to be amazingly unaware of the limitations of such data.

> One of the glaring problems in this connection is that of getting those who make educational decisions on the basis of test scores to realize that the best of achievement tests is never more than a sample of a student's performance and is therefore inevitably subject to sampling error. Another glaring problem in the interpretation of academic achievement tests has to do with the kinds of numbers in which the measures are customarily expressed—namely, so-called grade equivalency scores. Except for the notorious IQ, these are probably the most convenient devices ever invented to lead people into misinterpretations of students' test results. Both the IQ and grade equivalency scores are psychological and statistical monstrosities.

Here is how a grade equivalency score can lead a student astray (perhaps to his everlasting detriment).

Ralph, a sixth grader, takes a standardized reading achievement test the school has purchased from a publishing house. The testmaker determined through sampling a large number of sixth graders in different parts of the United States that average students at the beginning of the sixth grade score 40. This score is then assigned the grade equivalent of 6.0. Students who score higher than 40 go up a decimal ladder—6.1, 6.2, etc.; students with scores below 40 descend the ladder—5.9, 5.8, and so on.

Ralph's score is 26. On the decimal ladder descending from 6.0, the grade equivalent for the raw score of 26 is 4.1. It is reported that Ralph is reading at the level of a student in the first month of the fourth grade.

This simply is not so. The test only has indicated that in the sample taken of Ralph's reading performance he was below the average performance of sixth graders elsewhere. The grade equivalency score is, as Dr. Dyer said, a "psychological and statistical monstrosity."

Unfortunately for Ralph, his school and his parents, if they are told of his test score, falsely conclude that he is a fourth-grade reader, and he is subjected to a diet of fourth-grade books. The forced feeding of such inappropriate materials effectively kills Ralph's appetite for reading.

The test-makers, who know how great the margin of error can be in tests standardized for administration to masses of children, wonder how counselors and teachers can be so blind or so careless about their interpretation and application of test scores. Their smugness is a little hard to take since it is they who invented the monstrous language. These tests do not measure the learning, the progress, or the knowledge of an individual child. Strangely, instruments constructed to appraise large groups of children and make possible comparisons between the averages of whole schools and school systems with equivalent populations, never intended to be used in measuring and placing individual children, have been universally so used.

In any institution, adherence to its rules and customs is important. In guidance departments in schools the hidden rules are very important.

● The rule is that a student in the eighth grade will tell his counselor what he wants to be when he grows up and exits from formal education, and the counselor will write that goal at the top of a form that will follow the student through his senior year in high school.

The intent is that the career choice will help the counselor guide the student in his selection of high school courses. But no rule requires the counselor to become sufficiently interested in the student so that he is among the first to know when the student changes his career goal—the first time, the second time, and the third time.

As a matter of fact, the counselor is subtly encouraged to leave things as they are. For the hidden rule is that the institution will consider it disruptive if the student changes his mind and, therefore, his choices of courses not once but often. Such changes are normal and necessary in adolescence. But the institution approves what is abnormal.

● The rule is that in the early spring of each year of high school, until he is a senior, the student will select his courses for the following year according to what is prescribed by state law or local policy and from among available electives. Then the counselor will review his selections and send the prescribed form home with the student for his parents' review and signature.

The student elects not to take either algebra II or chemistry in his junior year, and the counselor writes a note to his parents at the bottom of the form sent home: "Without algebra II and chemistry, your son's choice of colleges is limited."

The counselor has adhered to the rule because that is how he gets along in the institution. But his note to the parents has served only to confuse them—and for several reasons:

1. Because the counselor seems not to have consulted at least the results of the one and only standardized test they have been informed about in nine years—the Differential Aptitude Test. The DAT clearly demonstrated to the parents (who had to interpret the results for themselves) that their son had a very low aptitude for math and science. And these findings have been corroborated consistently by the boy's very low marks in both subject areas.

2. Because the counselor has not defined for them what he means by a limited choice of colleges. Does he mean that their son cannot make it in the top 20 percent of the private colleges? Or 50 percent of all private and public colleges?

3. Because the counselor obviously had never asked their son in the last year what his plans were upon graduation from high school. If he had, he would have discovered that the boy is now considering three post-high school directions: voluntary military service, employment, and travel. College may come later, but it may be a community college.

These parents—and thousands like them across America—have had it.

They no longer will put up with the slow burn in their stomach when they ask their son for the thirty-fifth time why he's failing physics, and get no satisfactory response for the thirty-fifth time. They will not accept hypertension as the price they must pay to obtain satisfactory and complete answers to bona fide requests for information. In short, they are insisting that they and their children be treated as preferred clients.

Unfortunately, the guidance department incorporated into the school cannot oblige them. And neither can that latest addition to the counseling staff, the school psychologist.

The school psychologist's role in the school is a curious mixture resulting from the adaptation of part of his capabilities to the institution's view of his role. The schools require the services of a psychologist to satisfy state regulations that individual IQ tests be administered to certify a child's placement in a class for the mentally retarded. But since World War II the schools have also developed other reasons for wanting a psychologist.

Teachers and administrators have a real concern for children with emotional problems and behavioral disorders. Help is sought for the child whose erratic behavior upsets classroom and school decorum. In addition, there is a steady growth in teachers' awareness of the potential for mental illness in the overly quiet and withdrawn child.

So, the public's hope that psychologists might be helpful in the healthy development of children has been supported by the expectations of teachers and administrators. Unfortunately, the anticipated benefits from the psychologists' work have been seriously undercut by the mismatch between their training and the school as a setting for their work.

Psychologists are trained to analyze behavior and, given clinical experience, to understand the development of personality and to diagnose the sources of disruption that cause difficulties. The psychologist is trained to distinguish between the ordinary problems and the combination of symptoms that suggest serious illness.

If, after careful examination and study of a child, the psychologist makes a preliminary diagnosis of difficulty, he will recommend necessary therapy to the parents. He will refer the parents to a private practitioner or a public mental health clinic. But in many cases the parents can't afford the private practitioner and public assistance is not readily available. In such instances, the school psychologist must decide what he can do as an interim measure, or what total service he can provide as a substitute for the recommended therapy.

It is at this point that the institution begins to mold the psychologist to its ways. If the child were in need of an appendectomy, the school would refuse to sponsor the operation. But in the field of child behavior the school feels obliged to provide treatment, including in some school systems the issuance of tranquilizers to "disruptive" children.

So, psychologists for the past twenty years have improvised a service to the school that utilizes only one aspect of their training and competence.

Their training has historically emphasized therapy as a process between a patient and a professional. Group therapy has been generated in part because of economy and because it was recognized that the group itself could be instrumental in bringing about desirable change in behavior. But in either case, the therapy depends on the psychologist's recognition that the pliable element—the condition needing change—is inside the patient.

There is a growing awareness that aspects of an institution or a society might be the cause of the mental ills demonstrated by people within the institution or society. Consequently, there also is an awareness that therapy might better be directed toward changing those elements in the institution or society which induce disturbances in people, rather than toward changing the people.

In the school, however, the psychologist is employed to change children, to make them more pliable to control and more obedient to the rules of the institution. The school psychologist has not been hired to change the institution, or to even suggest such a thing.

Therefore, that part of the psychologist's training which calls on him to provide individual therapy coincides with the institution's desire to have him treat children with problems so that they might adapt to the conditions within the institution. This places the psychologist in the role of an analyst treating individual children (and sometimes their parents) over a period of months or years. The result is that the psychologist's time is taken up with such a practice, and the practice is limited by necessity to twenty or twenty-five children a year.

This role prevents the psychologist's potential effectiveness in helping scores of teachers and hundreds of children. His role also should be one of a social diagnostician examining the conditions, the rules, and the atmosphere of the institution. He should be able to look at the behavior of teachers as factors in the mental health of children and the teachers themselves. He should help the institution reconstitute itself for the sake of those who are in it. Then we would have a full exploitation of the science that could promise great results for many instead of so little results for so few.

But the task of giving the psychologist this new role in the school is nearly impossible under present circumstances. Two powerful forces are reinforcing each other. The institution's view of the psychologist's role fits the psychologist's own view of himself as being a therapist for individuals for at least a good part of his professional day.

In order to impel the necessary new functions for the psychologist that we have described, it is once again necessary to provide a new form where such functions might flourish. These new functions are not possible within the present form.

We propose a new form—a Community Guidance and Evaluation Center.

The functions of guidance and evaluation would be excised from the school and removed to the new center. Here, counselors, psychologists, psychometricians, statisticians, and ombudsmen would work under the overall governance of the new Education Assembly that would replace today's board of education, and under the immediate direction of a board of elected citizens and its executive officer.

In the old institution the student and his parents could not be served well because the implicit and explicit rules of the institution compelled counselors, psychologists, and teachers to believe and behave in ways which did not satisfy the needs of students and parents.

In our Community Guidance and Evaluation Center, the staff would find the rewards and sanctions directly related to serving clients—students and families. Counselors would discover that their training and their duties are at last in harmony. No longer would a counselor have to edit his responses to the needs of students because he is worried about the possible reactions of their teachers. No longer would a psychologist be required to elect the personal therapist role as his only resource for treating children.

In our center, the guidance counselors and other staff members would work for, and be responsible to, a board of citizens that would include parents. But the old institutional behavior that forced teachers and counselors to regard parents as enemies, or with defensiveness, no longer would be present. The counselor would be governed in his actions by his training, not by a complex patchwork of written rules and subliminal pressures that prevent him from doing for children that which he knows to be right.

Now, parents find it difficult, often impossible, to meet with those who should be able to tell them what they want and need to know about their children. Most cannot make an appointment at 9 A.M. or 3:35 P.M. And some of those who can, won't, because they are embarrassed or afraid.

Our Community Guidance and Evaluation Center would be open until late at night, many staff members having started the day at 2 or 3 P.M. Not only would parents be welcome, but the center's

staff actively would seek to advise them, to console them, to answer
their questions, to bring them understanding, and to listen to their
deepest expressions of desire and despair for their children.

If parents being served by the center are suspicious of any public
institution secure in its public building, staff members would go
out to meet parents assembled in the common room of a housing
development, in the fellowship hall of a neighborhood church, in
a storefront that is the focal point for community action and service. Our center not only is a place, it is a service.

If there are parents being served who speak no English, there
would be staff members available to communicate with them.

As an employee, the center staff member would be accountable
to the executive officer and the board of parents. But as a professional counselor, psychometrician, or ombudsman, he would be responsible to those students and parents who depend on him—his
preferred clients.

A student and his parents no longer would have to wonder and
speculate about the results of tests that measure his achievement
and learning ability. It would be incumbent upon the experts
manning the center to reveal the results, interpret them, and, most
important, to demonstrate how the data are being used for the
student's benefit.

Imagine now that it is tomorrow; our Community Guidance and
Evaluation Center is in business.

● Fred and his parents are meeting with Fred's counselor. It is
shortly after dinner on a Wednesday in mid-November. The reason
for the visit is that Fred is doing poorly in world history, a course
he had anticipated eagerly.

When Fred and his parents had worked out Fred's learning program last spring, the counselor had discussed different approaches
to learning in an effort to match Fred with programs and personnel
most apt to gain responses from this boy who tends to be sensitive
and shy.

Fred had heard from other students about a learning program
that demanded much individual investigation, group field work,
and lively group discussion.

The promise of individual investigation and group field work appealed to Fred, and he inadvertently overlooked the fact that dynamic debate was encouraged, an activity that might frighten a withdrawn boy like Fred.

Fred's records and the counselor's intimate knowledge of the boy told him that Fred needed a more structured learning environment and careful guidance. Fred's parents agreed with the counselor, but all decided to allow Fred to make his choice, thinking that perhaps Fred would overcome his shyness.

The counselor promised Fred and his parents last spring that the history specialists would be fully informed about Fred so that they might make Fred's experience as rewarding as possible. And the counselor said he would monitor Fred's progress every four weeks. The parents were to be sent a summary of the counselor's findings after each examination of Fred's progress.

Now, after both Fred and the history specialists have made a strong effort to make the learning experience pay off for Fred, they realize that it is not working satisfactorily *for Fred*. The counselor now suggests again that Fred take a history program more compatible with his learning style.

It is agreed that the transfer will be made the following Monday. Fred and his parents are delighted.

● The program for Alice calls for her to spend five hours a week at the local hospital. She has expressed an interest in medicine, and the hospital has agreed to give her the varied experiences that will help her determine whether she might like to make a career in medicine and, if so, in what capacity.

In early October, Alice complains to her parents that the hospital is not offering her the opportunities promised. She spends most of her five hours sitting in the nurses' lounge waiting for someone to give her something to do. The few chores she has had were sorting laundry and wheeling patients to and from a solarium. She has asked for more and varied work; she has asked people to demonstrate what they do—all to no avail.

Alice's mother calls the hospital but is unable to talk to anyone who can give her any satisfaction. Alice and her mother go to Alice's career supervisor. He also gets the runaround in several phone calls.

Finally, the career supervisor refers Alice and her mother to an ombudsman. The ombudsman is not an expert in counseling, testing, learning theories, or family relationships. But he has insight into all of these things. His special training is in advocacy, and he is able to analyze problems that divide people from people and people from institutions.

He is well acquainted with the leverage points not only in the other institutions for public education, but also in local government and industry. In short, he knows how to get things done.

The ombudsman interviews Alice, her mother, and the career supervisor to obtain all background data. He wants to know what the arrangement with the hospital is supposed to be, what it actually is, and what has happened to the mother and the supervisor in their efforts to get satisfaction.

The next day the ombudsman goes to the hospital. He bypasses all those whom he knows cannot help and will only ensnare him in red tape, and goes directly to the administrator with whom the arrangements for Alice (and other students) have been made.

The administrator obviously is unaware of what has happened. The complaints of Alice, her mother, and the supervisor have not reached him. He shows the ombudsman schedules he has made out for all students working at the hospital, including Alice. He has carefully planned a rich program for each person. Unfortunately, he has neglected to follow up his directions to subordinates to see if the programs are being carried out.

The hospital administrator and the career supervisor organize a better monitoring system that should insure that Alice and other students will have the experiences they have been promised. In two days Alice finds her work at the hospital has been increased and varied.

● A psychometrician at the center receives a report indicating that Philip, aged seven, has not mastered three or four initial reading skills. After an analysis of Philip's reading profile (including all past records), the psychometrician determines that out of the four skills Philip has not mastered, only one is critical to his further progress. The other three skills can be worked on later.

The psychometrician goes to Philip's counselor, and together they write a memorandum to the teacher responsible for Philip's reading instruction. It is suggested that Philip be given some drill in the one critical skill. The memo also asks for a re-evaluation of Philip's progress in reading after ninety days, the results to be sent to the psychometrician.

● Donna, who is thirteen, has expressed to her parents and to her counselor an interest in interior decorating as a *possible* career choice. She isn't old enough to work part time in the business; besides, she is not sufficiently mature to take on such a responsibility.

The center maintains what it calls the Greater Community Talent Bank. On file are names of persons in many different occupations. There are doctors, truck drivers, airplane pilots, architects, waitresses, policemen, actors, beauty technicians, nuclear scientists, landscapers, and so on. Everybody indexed has agreed to volunteer time occasionally to talk with interested students and take them to their job when possible.

Donna goes to the talent bank, which resembles a card catalog in a library. She finds cards on three interior decorators. She feels uncomfortable with male adults just now and rejects two of the three immediately. She takes the information on the card about the woman decorator to the counselor, who calls her on the telephone. An appointment is made for Donna and the woman to meet Saturday morning at the office/showroom of the decorator.

The Community Guidance and Evaluation Center also would be directed by legislation to be the the Price–Waterhouse for all of the new institutions for public education. Education would have an academic audit which would provide the kind of objective, expert evaluation of programs and personnel performance that is not now possible.

The center's experts are not on the staff, related to the staff, or beholden to the staff of any of the other institutions. Therefore, they are able to assemble, interpret, and accurately report objective and honest data. By reporting to the Education Assembly, the boards of each educational institution, and the general public, there could be no divided loyalties. The people are the clients of the Community Guidance and Evaluation Center.

On a cyclical basis, the center staff—again augmented by whatever professionals are needed—would review the five major areas of learning: mathematics, physical sciences, language arts, social sciences, and fine arts. Each major field would be thoroughly reviewed every five years and a report and recommendations prepared.

Part of these reports would entail a critical appraisal in cost-effectiveness terms of the benefits derived from one program versus others in the same field. Education badly needs an agency such as our center to measure and evaluate results independently. Such an appraisal might find, for instance, that of two good learning programs one costs less. Education always has had an institutional incapacity to understand that one of the most valuable findings can be evidence that a program should be stopped.

A periodic review of the social sciences might discover that most children have a poor understanding of geography. The center's report to the Education Assembly probably would suggest that the social sciences faculty make its own study and then offer a plan for correcting the apparent deficiency. The faculty's plan might include provisions for periodic evaluation of any suggested reforms.

While the assessment of what is happening in the various institutions for public education would be intended to help improve the programs offered, assessment reports would be summarized for wide public dissemination.

No longer would the public have to guess whether what it hears about the failings of foreign language laboratories is true. No longer would people have to wonder why the originators of the new math were disappointed in what happened to the innovation after it moved into the classroom. No longer would parents have to speculate about why some scholars say the Discovery Method in the social sciences is better than traditional approaches—and what the Discovery Method is.

If the language arts faculty want to experiment with new courses in literature, they would first consult with the center staff about the current state of performance by students in this area, the goals of the courses, and how progress toward these objectives and student learning would be evaluated.

The Education Assembly, by charging the Community Guidance and Evaluation Center with responsibility for auditing all activities that the various institutions under its control are engaged in, hopefully will eliminate forever an ancient abuse in American education. That is the practice of changing, adding, subtracting, and multiplying pieces of curriculum by guess and by golly, by wetting the finger to see how the winds of fad are blowing.

These two functions of the center—the guidance of people and the evaluation of programs—may in large population areas be partially separated. The guidance centers would occur as frequently as geographic distance and density of population require—perhaps one for every 40,000 or 50,000 persons. But the evaluation function is a service to the whole community through its representatives in the Education Assembly, and only one evaluation center would be required regardless of the size of the community.

Our Community Guidance and Evaluation Center also would forever wipe away the ancient and utterly inane practice of measuring the quantity and quality of an individual's learning solely according to what courses he took, how many Carnegie units (credit hours) he compiled, what marks were recorded for him, and what class rank was assigned him.

The center's concern would be to measure the individual's real learning and real competence. It would not be concerned at all with where the individual learned and gained his competency.

- Because the individual might have learned to type fifty words per minute from his mother, a former secretary.
- Because the individual might have learned the equivalent of college freshman geology during eight years of devoted study and exploration with a rock-collecting club.
- Because the individual might have learned to read without ever coming within a block of a school.

● Because the individual might have become a master artist by observing and working alongside her grandfather.

● Because the individual might have learned basic chemistry at a three-week summer workshop on water pollution.

The fact that a student has completed algebra II is meaningless. What is important is whether he can demonstrate sufficient proficiency in mathematics to qualify him for the college program or career he has chosen. A year in Europe can be an educational experience or a mixed bag from psychedelic tripping. An individual might learn more about Shakespeare's plays by watching a dozen of them played than by spending a year reading two of them and listening to others talk about them.

The center would measure learning and competency only for its clients—students, their parents, and other residents of the community it serves. Results of examinations to determine mastery of knowledge or skills would be turned over to the clients directly, not admissions officers, personnel managers, hiring bosses, or employment agencies.

The clients, of course, could take the results wherever they wished, using them as evidence of their ability to meet the standards of the keeper of the gates at the college, the business, or the union.

By riveting its attention and its concern on its clients, the center does not risk becoming the servant of the college admissions office, the industry, or the union. Today's complaint that high school guidance counselors work harder at selecting students for colleges and jobs than they do at finding the right colleges and jobs for students is not without substance.

We expect the Community Guidance and Evaluation Center to be the militant spokesman for its clients who are denied entry into the world of higher education and the world of work because of irrelevant and indefensible standards.

The center would object to its clients being denied admission or employment because schools, colleges, employers, and government agencies refuse to accept indications of proficiencies or competencies measured at the center in ways different from the usual practice. We are so accustomed to measuring indirectly the symptoms of competence that we seldom question the validity of the measurement. We accept a diploma as an indicator of quality, courses taken for knowledge acquired, time spent for skills mastered.

Learning can take place other than in a school and over different lengths of time other than five forty-minute periods every week, or a semester. Direct measurement of skills desired by employers, while difficult, are more reliable and are essential if we are to free the processes of learning from the strictures of existing school forms.

The center's role would not be unlike that of the American Civil Liberty Union's when people are denied rights, privileges, and opportunities because of their race, sex, or religion.

● The center would complain loudly against colleges who will accept as evidence of presumed proficiency only the standard measures such as transcripts recording courses taken, grades received, and rank in class. Because the student who takes and passes the courses only proves that he has taken and passed the courses. He has not proved competency. The center would provide evidence of competency achieved in a variety of unorthodox ways for its clients to use at their discretion. The center would argue that college entrance requirements be both more specific and more appropriate for the student's intended course of study.

● The center would complain loudly against employers who ask only that applicants produce evidence of a high school diploma certifying that they have successfully completed formal schooling. If the center could furnish its clients evidence of the competency needed for the job, no matter how it was learned, the clients—and the center—would insist on their eligibility. The center would argue (and on the foundation laid down by recent court decisions) that the diploma as an exclusive standard of employability is meaningless as a measure of learning or competence, and that employers must set entry standards that are realistic for the demands of the job to be performed. If the employer can justify saying that basic accounting is a necessary beginning skill for the job open, then the center would supply its clients test data descriptive of the proficiency in that field.

- The center would complain loudly against the college or employer who demanded of one of its clients that he reveal where his learning took place, and then used such information as grounds for rejecting him. If the boy learned typing from his mother, the former secretary, instead of in a classroom, that must not be held against him any more than the fact that he is male, black, and a charter member of the Jesus People.

We believe that the removal of guidance, testing, and evaluation from the graded and appended school and the creation of an autonomous Community Guidance and Evaluation Center would greatly improve American public education if nothing else were ever accomplished.

But when this critical operation was sketchily outlined before a group of high school students, a girl raised a complaint: "Guidance counselors are remote now; they'll be even more remote if they're in another place."

There are two kinds of remoteness—between people and distance. The girl probably passed the guidance office at least once a day for 180 school days every year; she was that close to it. But her counselor saw her only once a year—at his invitation. She was not remote from the guidance office, but she was terribly remote from her counselor.

At our Community Guidance and Evaluation Center, students, parents, and other community residents may have to walk or ride blocks to the center, but they never will be remote from their counselors, the ombudsmen, and the other members of the staff.

Preferred clients just aren't treated that way.

Four

To Your Family's Good Health

A KINDERGARTNER TURNS UP HIS FACE to the teacher and asks, "When am I going to be big?"

Twelve years and umpteen gym periods later, a high school senior complains to his physical education and health teachers, "You never taught me about my body. Not really. I remember once one of you showed off by reciting the Latin names of the bones in our legs and arms. But you were as bad as our supposedly modern parents when it came to menstruation, sex, and keeping clean."

The kindergartner and the senior are among 5,000 students in Connecticut questioned in 1967–1968 about their health interests and concerns. The survey report[1] stated: "The extent and depth of the interest in health exceeded all expectations. Children express deep need to understand their own development, and from grades five or six on, they feel handicapped and often at a loss at not understanding. It is as though they said, 'It is we who must manage our lives. Adults, please tell us how we grow, so that we in turn may tell you what we need to know in order to act as self-directing, responsible people.' "

Why do children feel "handicapped?" Why does a senior feel cheated after twelve long years of physical education and health instruction? Because once again performance has run twenty laps behind good intention. The graded and appended school has professed

1. Ruth V. Byler, Gertrude M. Lewis, and Ruth J. Totman, *Teach Us What We Want to Know* (Connecticut State Board of Education, 1969).

69

concern for the individual's physical development and good health, but its program in both fields has been designed for large masses of children in straitjackets called grades one, two, three, and so on.

In a 1965 statement on what physical education is (or is supposed to be), the American Association for Health, Physical Education, and Recreation (AAHPER) said:

> Provision for individual differences in ability and interest is an important principle in curriculum organization. In physical education, the 'slow growers' and 'fast growers' may well have special needs within the structure of their own age group.
>
> Children handicapped by structural, functional, or intellectual limitations need specially adapted exercises, games, and dances that may be quite different from those suited to the needs of their more fortunate peers. Similarly, those gifted in the ability to coordinate their own movements may profit from participation in more complex activities.

Outlining what the school says it does for the individual's health, Professors Helen Norman Smith and Mary E. Wolverton[2] said: "Individual school health services include all that happens to a child in order to determine his health status and to guide him in his individual development. Health appraisal of children is used as the basis for guiding school activity, for prevention or correction of defects and diseases, for individual counsel, and for general emphasis in health instruction."

But the graded school is seldom able to make good on the promises to serve the individual. Listen again to the children of Connecticut as they ask their unanswered questions and express their unfulfilled needs year after year after year.

- Grade three: "How do I grow?" "Does my heart look like a valentine?"
- Grade four: "What makes the body grow?" "I am nine years old and small. Do you think I will be six feet tall?"
- Grade five: "How does a body grow?" "Why are some people smaller than others?"

2. Helen Norman Smith and Mary E. Wolverton, *Health Education in the Elementary School* (New York: Ronald Press Co., 1959).

- Grade eight: "What makes you grow fat?" "How can I take weight off quickly?" "How can I lose weight on food I like?"
- Grade ten: "Why don't we have a health club where we can build up our bodies?" "Who needs the most exercise?"
- Grade eleven: "Why do people hide sex, if it is good and natural?" "Should I use diet pills?" "We should do things we can use in the future."

While each child ponders the host of mysteries about his body and muses over how best to use it and take care of it, the institution is otherwise engaged.

- "All right, when I blow the whistle, everybody run around the track three times."
- "Everybody place their hands on their hips. Now, when I begin the count, first touch your left knee with your right elbow, then the right knee with the left elbow. Keep your legs straight. Okay, by the numbers . . ."
- "Today, we're all going to draw posters for Dental Health Week."
- "If someone will please get the lights, I'm going to run a film on the dangers of smoking."
- "Now, everyone line up so the doctor can check you over. Boys go in this line and girls go over there. Boys, open your shirts."

The AAHPER said in 1970 that the physical education program in the elementary grades "serves the divergent needs of all pupils . . . and is geared to the developmental needs of each child."

But, in fact, across the face of America physical education in grades one through six is mainly a matter of the most able and most extroverted choosing up sides for team play at recess, and the less able either learning America's most popular sport—watching—or playing in twos and threes. The teacher's role is as arbiter of disputes and preventer, insofar as it is possible, of skinned knees, cut fingers, and torn clothing.

Indeed, the institution shows plainly how it regards physical education in the elementary grades when it sanctions the use of mothers as playground aides. The institution assumes that an untrained person probably can serve just as well as the supervisor for the children's spontaneous play.

We don't mean to deprecate the happy tradition called recess. For many children there are more physical and social benefits to be derived from free play on the playground or in the gymnasium than in the mass activities misnamed physical education. But we do submit that the school does not honor its commitment to serve "the divergent needs of all pupils" when in the name of a physical education program it requires of its teachers only that they break up fights and guard against accidents.

The teacher in the elementary grades is asked to make sure that Shirley and Danny don't battle each other or someone else, that they don't go down the slide head first or stand too close to a swinging batter. But this teacher who is chiefly responsible for "the developmental needs of each child" is not asked to notice or care that Shirley never participates and that Danny's weight is a drag both medically and socially.

There are elementary schools, of course, where organized physical education is provided—once, twice, maybe even three times a week. But it is the rare physical education instructor who does more than impose and direct mass play or calisthenics only remotely or accidentally appropriate for the growth of Shirley or Danny.

To begin with, the physical education instructor sees children in graded packages and in large numbers—fifty to one hundred at one time not being uncommon. He is expected to assume, as is every other teacher of every other subject in the graded school, that those exercises and games prescribed for third graders (or eight-year-olds) are right for all third graders (or eight-year-olds).

Like the classroom teacher, the physical education instructor is neither encouraged nor rewarded for diagnosing and treating individual needs—whether they are Shirley's, Danny's, or anyone else's.

He *is* encouraged and rewarded, however, if he spots and then cultivates students—particularly boys—who can be turned over to the coaches in the later grades.

The August 15, 1970 issue of *Physical Education Newsletter*[3] devoted two of its four pages to a discussion of an "entire curriculum guide" designed to impart soccer skills to children in grades four through six. "Soccer is a prime fall physical education activity for boys and girls beginning in the intermediate grades," the article began.

But we ask, what in the world does the instep kick, the inside-the-foot kick, and the outside-the-foot kick have to do with "the developmental needs of each child"? Will mass instruction in dribbling and the thigh trap serve the needs of Shirley? Danny?

It seems clear that sports as a means have become in the minds of many physical education instructors in our schools ends in themselves. It is assumed beyond question that mass participation in sports and drill in skills will produce physically able children. But the means are remote from the ends. The program works only for the athletically elite.

And because the institution rewards its coaches as the adult stars of the physical education program, sports and the early discovery and training of the biologically gifted become the central purposes of the physical education teachers.

The institution's primary justification for three years' worth of instruction in soccer skills (five weeks per year) apparently was spelled out by the curriculum expert for physical education in the district concerned: "The new guide helped us to do a better job of teaching fundamentals and preparing students for advanced soccer in the secondary grades."

The AAHPER's position paper on physical education in the elementary school contains a section on evaluation. "Evaluation must be a continuous and vital part of the physical education program," says the paper. "It is used to determine and clarify instructional purposes and to assess individual pupil progress in achieving program objectives."

Again, the words are very nice. But the actual practice is something else. Does any parent in the United States expect—or receive

3. *Physical Education Newsletter* (New London, Conn.: Croft Educational Services, 1970).

—from the school an evaluation of his child's "progress in achieving program objectives" in physical education? The strangely lethargic Shirley and obese Danny are promoted into next year's group sports and exercises, which they will find just as useless and just as frustrating year after year after year.

It would be a rare occurrence if a classroom teacher in the elementary grades discussed a child's physical development in a conference with a parent, except perhaps to comment that "Shirley's going through a stage," or "Danny's a big boy for his age." First of all, the teacher is not held responsible for being concerned or keeping track of an individual's physical development, and neither is the physical education instructor. And there are no conferences with the physical education instructor in any event. Most parents would be hard-pressed to name their child's "gym teacher."

The "continuous and vital" evaluation then turns out to be little more than a Field Day blue ribbon or a Presidential Physical Fitness Award for the exceptionally gifted, and for everybody a notation on the report card that reads something like this: "A program in physical education is presented on each grade level. Your child's work may be considered satisfactory if no comment is made."

There almost never is a comment, unless the child has been "disruptive" because he failed to follow orders, beat up on other children, or violated the rules governing proper use of the equipment.

In the secondary grades of the graded school, physical education is more organized and offered more regularly. But it is just more of the same, except that now students must do more exercises and do them for a longer period. And for a very few, the "coach" observes their promise for varsity sports and undertakes to turn them into public performers on the field or court.

The institution makes it very clear to the male physical education teachers in the secondary grades that they will be accorded higher status and additional compensation if they coach winning sports teams. They will gain no extra rewards from the institution for serving the physical developmental needs of individual children. The students suppose that physical education is intended to develop their body, but they rarely take it seriously because they know how the institution and their teachers regard it.

- The institution says that what's important in school is what gets you into college or into a good job. Physical education is not on that list.

- If a student is not on a team, or in the running for one, the instructors will not be especially concerned whether he has developed muscle tone, improved his posture, licked his weight problem, overcome his awkwardness, or learned to enjoy a physical game or skill that will stand him in good stead as a man of middle age.

- The student is assured of a good mark—the symbol of success in American education—if he causes no trouble. In fact, a high school physical education teacher told his boys they would all receive at least a B unless they missed taking showers.

But the students know what their physical education teachers do take seriously: the protesting minority that "forgets" sneakers, takes home uniforms to be washed only to have mother "forget" to do it, or develops disabling aches and pains on the way to the locker room.

The teacher's hostility ("If I've told you guys once, I've told you a thousand times . . .") is in direct proportion to his recognition that the kids are telling him that his program is crud.

It is true that some kids malinger because of physical awkwardness and shame at not being able to perform like the gifted. But more do it as a statement of their feeling that physical education is worthless. And no teacher, even a bad one, can easily accept being told he is useless.

The evidence is decisive. No class in any subject is so frequently a target of skipping and truancy than boys' and girls' high school physical education.

If the public schools of the United States were to adopt as policy that only the most gifted in math would receive the full attention of the math teacher, that only those who showed exceptional skill in English would get more than token instruction from the English teacher, parents from coast to coast would join in a crescendo of protest.

But from sea to shining sea, the overwhelming majority of boys and girls are routinely eliminated from the only physical education programs that devote any particular attention to individual body development. They are eliminated every time a coach posts the names of the gifted who have elected and then carefully been selected to receive special attention as members of a team.

The American people must understand—and be revolted by— this system that places a higher value on winning teams than on the physical development of each child as advocated by the American Association for Health, Physical Education, and Recreation. The American people must know—and be shocked by the fact— that conforming physical education teachers, conserving their energy until they meet their team after school, figuratively and literally walk away from the needs of most of the other children in their care from 8:30 A.M. to 3 P.M.

It may be that a sports program and a physical education program for all children can be effective under the same roof in the same institution, and be operated by the same adults. But there is no evidence in the American public schools that would indicate that this is so. What we have, instead, is an excellent sports program for the few and a remarkably poor, or even nonexistent, physical education program for the many.

The schools do only a so-so job with the three Rs. They fail miserably when teaching the three Ds—diet, dexterity, and development.

Traditionally, the United States has become alarmed when 25 percent or more of its young men do not qualify physically for the draft. What a tragedy that as a people we are concerned that so many youths are unfit to kill or be killed, but remain mostly unconcerned over the school system's inability to reduce the huge numbers of the unfit.

And while the American taxpayer lately has pinched his pennies when asked to build rooms for reading, painting, and making music, he has almost never questioned the lavish costs of the sports program and its attending arenas. How extraordinary a world it would be if fathers organized as boosters for boys who would be poets, and mothers sat on the sidelines to cheer little leagues of artists or musicians.

Almost every traditional elementary and secondary school includes a gymnasium with a ceiling twenty or more feet high. Such a cavernous room is not designed to meet the physical education needs of individual children. It is designed for only one thing—basketball. Almost all other indoor activities that young people might engage in to improve their body development can be accommodated easily in rooms of considerably reduced dimensions.

For example, the ceiling in a room where indoor physical education other than basketball can take place could easily be kept below fourteen feet. The extra footage is a mammoth investment so that ten can be watched by hundreds. But at least the gymnasium is frequently used by physical education classes (although the extra space is inappropriate for their needs). The football stadium, on the other hand, is almost an exclusive sanctuary for the varsity team.

Swimming is a good body-builder and a recreational activity which can be engaged in long after men have given up shooting baskets and going for the TD and women have turned their back on field hockey and softball. Yet, there is no pool in most school systems; indeed, there are no public pools in most communities.

Why? Many persons say a pool is a "frill" the school system cannot possibly afford. But it is much less a frill to the school system than the high-domed gym for varsity basketball or the stadium reserved for varsity football. And a pool can be used day and night, winter and summer, for all ages.

Basketball and football are both exciting spectator sports, considerably more so than swimming. They both take in big money at the gate—whether the gate belongs to a midwestern high school or a big league syndicate. But we thought the AAHPER was talking about meeting the developmental needs of all children, not just those who excel at layups, set shots, broken field running, blocking, and passing.

One might logically assume that if the school were right, then the gym, the football stadium, and the baseball diamond would satisfy both the developmental and recreational needs of youth. But consider as exhibit one in this case against the graded and appended school the following evidence from a survey of teenagers in typical middle-class America.

Midland Park, New Jersey, is populated by slightly more than 8,000 persons, not a few of whom are descended from early Dutch settlers. Situated about twenty miles northwest of Times Square, the town is almost exclusively residential. There are two elementary schools and a junior-senior high school occupying slightly more than twenty-seven acres in the small community.

In 1970, a research team composed of students from the Bureau of Applied Social Research at Columbia University, the New York State University at Stony Brook, and Harvard University made a survey and issued a report called "Student Views of Life in Midland Park." The report went to the community's Youth Commission.

"When asked if there was anything that they would like to do that they cannot do in Midland Park," said the report, "69 percent said yes, and 58 percent of those mentioned some kind of sport. Of those who mentioned sports, nearly half said swimming." The report went on:

> . . . Most students felt that the facilities for sports are inadequate. Although swimming is very popular, there is no town pool. A pool is the most obvious example, but students list a number of other sports-related facilities that they would like to have in the town, such as a bowling alley, a minibike track, and a multipurpose recreation center.

Most of the young people of Midland Park found that athletic facilities in town were inadequate, despite the hundreds of thousands of dollars spent on gymnasiums and playing fields. And the reason so many found the facilities inadequate is that they were not appropriate to the needs of most kids at the time of the survey, and they certainly will not be appropriate to their needs as men and women. By advocating building a pool and bowling alley, the students demonstrated they had a much clearer vision of their requirements for the future than did the institution in town that was conceived and dedicated to preparing them for the future. Of course, we're speaking of the school system.

Not only are schools in Midland Park and all over the United States failing to pay attention to individual needs for body development through physical education, they are also failing to fulfill the promise to America's children made by the pedagogues of health education.

What schools sponsor active clubs in hiking, bicycling, walking, exploring, climbing? How many offer golfing or tennis to more than a few kids?

Helen Norman Smith and Mary E. Wolverton, professors of physical and health education, said only twelve years ago that "individual school health services include all that happens to a child in order to determine his health status and to guide him in his individual development. Health appraisal of children is used as the basis for guiding school activity, for prevention or correction of defects and diseases."

Unfortunately, once again, school life as it is supposed to be has been confused with defacto school life. What penalties children have paid through the generations because America's educators could not tell the difference.

The truth is that what "happens to a child in order to determine his health status" is not of much consequence for the vast majority of children.

The schools are mostly concerned with the well-being of those organs deemed necessary to pursuing the institution's proffered program—the eyes and the ears. But the remainder of children's bodies are generally ignored, so long as the bodies are warm.

In order for the student to get what the graded school is giving, he must be able to read books and see the blackboard, listen to the teachers' lectures and orders, and take notes and tests. The institution's primary concern about children's health, therefore, is that they can see, listen, and write.

The school system has been quite persistent for some time in the detection of eye difficulties. More recently, many systems have begun audiometer testing of children's hearing.

For those students with bad eyes, corrective glasses are recommended. And the school recommends hearing aids or speech therapy (which it may provide) for those youngsters whose audiometer tests reveal severe handicaps related to hearing. But minor hearing deficiencies may go undetected, or may be only noted clerically and then overlooked by the school because it is assumed that the defect will not prevent the student from communicating with the teacher.

The institution's very limited interest in children's health, except as it may be deemed to interfere with acceptance of the instructional program designed for the masses, is clearly demonstrated by the use of results of audiometer examinations and the consequences for children.

A child's hearing test results may indicate that he will have no difficulty hearing lectures and orders and making the proper responses, but the child still may be greatly handicapped in school. Reading expert Helen Robinson[4] says that "high frequency losses among retarded readers may be undetected and may limit skill in phonetic analysis of words." Since the preponderance of research points to competency in phonetics as the key to learning to read, it is quite possible that many poor readers are handicapped by minor deficiencies in hearing that go uncorrected because the school has never thought them important enough from its standpoint to do anything about.

The real tragedy for children is not that educators still do not have all the answers about the relationship between hearing and reading; it is that the institution has not even thought it important to demand the research.

But the school has only a slight institutional concern for the

4. Helen Robinson, *Yearbook No. 40, Part I* (Chicago: National Society for the Study of Education, 1961).

state of health of the remainder of the child's body. After all, the boy or girl with early signs of curvature of the spine can still function as a student on the terms established by the institution.

Consequently, if the school system pays any attention at all to a child's general physical well-being it is usually for the sake of detecting and cataloging defects, especially if such a collection of data is required by local or state health and education authorities.

The defects noted are those that are obvious—a severe limp, disfigurement, etc.—and those that can be detected in an occasional once-over-lightly examination by the school physician. Children are run through these examinations like cars in an assembly line. In most instances, the doctor's examination consists of less than ninety seconds' worth of above-the-waist testing with the stethoscope (over clothes) and a fast look at the eyes, ears, and throat. It is to the credit of many physicians—with no credit to the schools at all—that there is as much diagnosis of physical defects and poor health as there is.

But most imperfections and signs of poor health are simply noted by the schools and, if required, reported to higher authorities for inclusion in unused archives. Superintendents file annual reports with their state education departments listing typically as many as 10 percent of the children having one or more physical defects. The catalogs are prepared by the nursing staff in each school district and turned over to the superintendent for his automatic, no-questions-asked signature.

If a superintendent should ask if anything is being done to remediate any child's problem, he usually is told that this child and that one have been excused from physical education. The answer might just as well be "No."

Classroom instruction about health often is dominated by lectures and films about the dangers of alcohol, nicotine, venereal diseases, and narcotics. Most of the instruction has had little effect on the incidence of alcoholism, smoking, gonorrhea and syphilis, and drug abuse.

Beginning in 1872 in Ohio, under pressure from the Woman's Christian Temperance Union, the schools began telling children about the evils of hard liquor. The instruction was intended more to scare the dickens out of them than to inform them with facts and answer their real questions. The schools have been at it ever since 1872.

But early in 1971 the United States Department of Health, Education and Welfare reported that there were 9 million problem drinkers in the country, that alcoholism is the number three killer, and that one out of every fourteen workers in America is an alcoholic (and cost the businesses they work for up to $4 billion a year).

Much of the health education has been a failure simply because it was moralistic propaganda and was seen for what it was by the majority of students. They had questions and concerns about their body and their health—like those expressed by the children in Connecticut—but health teachers provided few answers and remedies.

Another reason why the preaching lessons on alcohol and smoking have had little or no effect is that American society has accepted, and our children have learned, that alcohol drinking and cigarette smoking are true marks of growing up—insignia of adulthood.

It was to be a man or a woman to drink beer, or sip a highball, or smoke a cigarette. And American industry found it exceptionally profitable to promote their consumption. A boy could be a real man in Marlboro Country and a girl could come a long way with Virginia Slims.

One generation ago, when the schools exhorted children to brush their teeth daily and wash their bodies more frequently than Saturday night, big business gave support to these teachings. The soap and toothpaste industries advertised heavily to educate the American consumer. It was a Procter & Gamble morality that profited everybody—including children.

The school's failure or success at changing health behavior largely has been determined by the decisions made in executive suites and advertising agencies.

Most states have enacted laws that require a certain number of hours per year of instruction in physical education and health, and in some states courses are even dictated. The legislation, plus the rhetoric by such educational authorities as the American Association for Health, Physical Education, and Recreation, are all calculated to assure the parents of the United States that the schools are serving individual children's physical development and health needs.

Lamentably, it is a grossly false assurance. And the children of America—and their parents—deserve something better than a false assurance that everything is being done, when in fact in its scope and consequences the school's effort is significantly closer to being insignificant.

The physical education program does not respond to students' real needs, and the schools regrettably have confused sports with physical education. Most of children's health defects go unattended, and youngsters with physical limitations remain limited. Health education may sometimes be moralistic, but is seldom realistic. It is almost always inadequate.

It is our opinion that only small gains can be made by tinkering with the existing structure for providing physical education and health services. Therefore, we advocate as the "something better" a new public institution called the Family Health Center.

At the same time that physical and health education are excised from the school to be transplanted into the Family Health Center, the school's elaborate and costly sports program would be moved to where it has always rightfully belonged—under the sponsorship of the community recreation agency.

Those boys and girls who have the ability for and the interest in competitive sports—whether it be football, baseball, basketball, swimming, field hockey, or something else—should have full opportunity to join teams and play other teams. Those men and women now on the physical education faculty of schools, whose primary or favored employment is coaching such sports teams, would follow the sports program and become employees of the municipal recreation agency.

We will shout siss-boom-bah as loudly as anyone for our favorite team. But we prefer that in the future our heroes do or die for the glory of the old town rather than the old school.

Incidentally, with the sports program under the competent

direction of the municipal recreation agency, the municipal governing body or the recreation agency itself would have full responsibility for the maintenance of existing school gymnasiums and
stadiums that would be used primarily or solely for the sports teams
under the control of the recreation agency. Of course, future construction of facilities designed to serve the exclusive needs of the
sports program also would be the responsibility of the municipality.

We do not wish, nor do we think it possible, to improve upon
recess as a welcome break in the day's routine (although we sincerely
hope that each student's day in the future will be less routine and
considerably more rewarding and exhilarating). In fact, we would
extend the concept of free time for games and other wholesome
pastimes of their choice to older students.

There is no reason why children of all ages should not have time
during the day when they can play a pickup game of baseball or
football, fly a kite, whittle a stick, chat with friends, jump rope,
daydream, ride a bike, or just stretch to unwind anything that's
uptight.

But we would not consider recess, or the break in the day's
activities, to be an adequate physical education. So, the program
that would serve the individual child's physical development and
health needs would be directed by the Family Health Center.

The center probably would be under the direction of public
health and medical authorities, although in some areas our proposed Education Assembly might have to create the Family Health
Center. In any event, the Education Assembly would want to cooperate closely with municipal health authorities to assure that the
center meets the needs of children.

For example, ground was broken in February 1971 for the first
of five new family health care centers in the Bronx, New York.
Gordon Chase, the health services administrator for New York City,
described the centers as being designed to offer total health care
for families in the neighborhoods served. "A lot of people in the
Bronx, in New York State, and across the country only see a doctor
when they're critically ill or injured," said Chase. "The idea [of
the centers] is to provide the kind of health care which will keep

families well, instead of patching them up when they get in trouble."

Our Family Health Center would be concerned with monitoring regularly the total physical development and health of all members of families being served, not examining just the eyes and the ears of students. And it would work to *correct* defects, not just to count them and send the data off to the state capital for preservation in neglected files.

On the staff of the Family Health Center would be the professionals now employed by the schools but used exceptionally ineffectively for improving the physical development and health of individuals. The staff would include, then, physical education instructors, physicians, nurses, some psychologists, and social workers.

Added to the staff of the health center would be dentists, medical assistants, and ombudsmen. The ombudsmen would play a role similar to the one played by their counterparts in the Community Guidance and Evaluation Center: making the system work for people. Some staff members—particularly some physicians and dentists—would work part time at the center.

The health center is not a new approach to socialized medicine. Families who desire private medical examination and treatment, and can afford it, would be encouraged to pursue that course. Our intention is not to conceive of an institution that would supplant effective private medical practice. We are proposing a new institution to take over *from the school* those responsibilities for physical education and health it has assumed, or had imposed upon it, but has implemented badly.

Of course, we have included the whole family in our new Family Health Center because we feel we have learned a lesson that the schools should have learned long ago: the life of the child cannot be considered apart from the life of the family of which he is a member.

The school takes a child through twelve years of schooling with only occasional—and usually superficial—consultations with and accountings to the child's parents along the way. We have tried to correct this fault in the Community Guidance and Evaluation Center.

When the school shows concern for the child's physical development and health—and we have shown how unconcerned the school can be—it pays almost no attention to the significant effect the child's life outside of school has on his physical development and health. To correct this fault is an important reason for involving the family.

Parents who are themselves in poor health, who eat and drink unwisely, who do not understand the importance of personal hygiene, who do not know what physical fitness means and how it is maintained are not likely to cooperate with the center to improve the physical development and health of their children.

The center would be responsible for diagnosing the overall needs for physical development and good health, recommending treatment as indicated, and providing as necessary an ombudsman to push and shove to get the needed treatment. Here's how it would work.

● Jane is fifteen; she would be considered normal and healthy in every school in the United States today. She always has the sniffles, but is rarely out sick with a cold. Her eyes look tired. And there is a slight sag in that sack of skin and bones that depends on good muscle tone to hold it firm and erect.

Jane's poor muscle tone and body grace are concerns of the Family Health Center; so is her chronic fatigue. After a careful examination and interview, the center calls Jane and her parents in for a conference.

The physicians of our health center would not see a child just when she and her parents know, or suspect, that she has an illness or is injured. And their concern would go beyond prescribing treatment for a specific sickness or injury. So, the physician meeting with Jane and her family has consulted with other members of the staff. It is their joint recommendation that Jane increase her sleeping time from seven to eight or nine hours per night, and that she begin eating breakfast regularly; that she meet with a physical education instructor every other day for a half hour at a time to run through certain exercises designed to improve her muscle tone and reverse the tendency toward round shoulders; that she meet once a week in the evening for at least two months with a psychologist—one employed by the center or one of her parents' choosing. The psychologist is suggested because it seems that Jane has a poor self-image that may be causing her to ignore her physical needs. Or, the psychologist might discover that her physical condition is the cause of poor self-esteem.

Jane and her parents immediately agree to most of the recommendations, but reserve judgment on meeting with the psychologist. The center cannot, and does not, compel people to make decisions or take actions with which they are uncomfortable. However, the assigned ombudsman would be concerned with Jane and would again call upon the parents in the near future to report on her progress.

● Walter is eight years old and obese. At the urging of a health center ombudsman, his parents take him to their physician for a thorough examination. The doctor reports to the parents and to the ombudsman that the boy's overweight is not caused by a medical problem; he prescribes a low-calorie diet and suggests more exercise.

On a week night at seven o'clock, Walter and his parents meet with the ombudsman and a physical education instructor at the health center. (The center would be open during the week until 10 P.M. and all day on the weekend.) The ombudsman goes over the doctor's report with the family.

Walter's parents want to help, but his mother, who is herself chubby, is not sure that she can change the family's menu to accommodate Walter. "I serve a lot of potatoes because we all like them," she says, "and I've always baked a cake or a pie at least twice a week for my family. My mother did it before me." The ombudsman says he can arrange for a dietician to talk with Walter's mother about different menus that might appeal to the family and help the boy's problem at the same time.

The physical education instructor makes two recommendations in line with the doctor's report: Walter should report to the health center daily for special reducing exercises, and he should engage frequently in active games of his choice.

Walter agrees to come to the center for the exercises, but he is hesitant about engaging in games. "I don't want other kids to laugh at me," he says. The physical education instructor tells him that there is a group of children with weight problems who regularly get together for swimming in the center's pool, hiking, and a variety of games. The teacher offers to introduce Walter to the group if he's interested.

Walter's interested.

● At age fourteen, George suffers from severe acne on his face. One of his teachers thinks the condition is causing George to be extremely self-conscious. She passes the information on to an ombudsman, who in turn asks George and his parents to visit him at the health center.

The parents inform the ombudsman that they cannot afford a doctor's visit just to "see about something as common as pimples." (To George, of course, the affliction is worse than the bubonic plague.) The ombudsman finally convinces George's parents to allow the boy to be examined by a center physician. The doctor at the clinic prescribes medication for George and a diet that restricts his intake of certain foods and drinks. In the course of his examination, the doctor notices that George's teeth are in poor condition, and he suggests to the parents that they take George to a center dentist.

The doctor reports back to the ombudsman, who calls George's parents to arrange a visit to a dentist. The center dentist recommends immediate attention to the boy's teeth and gums, and he offers the parents the names of several private dentists who might perform the work.

The ombudsman, who is as concerned with George's health as the ombudsman at the guidance center is concerned with his academic progress, makes a note to keep in touch with the parents.

Health education for children would be under the overall supervision and guidance of the center staff, although teachers naturally would be included in the program, as would outside experts from time to time. The outside experts would include such persons as a biochemist, neurologist, professor of anatomy at a nearby medical school, and nutritionist.

The curriculum would de-emphasize mass instruction on social problems and focus on the concerns and questions children have about themselves and others. The learning would be built more around such interests as those expressed by the children of Connecticut. Instead of innumerable lectures and movies there would be more group discussions and individual counseling. A sensitive teacher or nurse, for instance, would sense when it might be appropriate to invite a student in for a private talk.

Today's youths wear their hair long, and it infuriates many parents. What young people don't need, then, are sermons from teachers or nurses implying the evils of wearing hair long. But they probably would appreciate and benefit from professional advice, based on facts, concerning the importance of keeping hair clean, out of eyes, and so on. Instead of parental complaints about overindulgence in cola products, there would be data on the contents of cola and what effect an excessive intake of these contents might have upon the body.

In the past, our children and young people have asked about their body development and their health, and the graded and appended school has had few satisfactory answers.

In the past, the graded and appended school has not detected many of the health problems affecting children and youths, and has not always sought correction of those imperfections and abnormalities discovered in perfunctory examinations.

In the past, health education has meant lectures and films rather than frank discussions and learning about subjects of most concern to children and young people.

That's why we are convinced that physical education and health services must be removed from the school, where they have been malfunctioning appendages, and made to work effectively for individuals through the Family Health Center.

And that's why we would strip the school of the sports program and put it where it belongs in the community, where it can't be confused with physical education and body development for all.

Five

The Arts Are for Everybody

As USUAL, THE PEDAGOGUES' INTENTIONS were right when they introduced the arts into the school. If Man is to be truly fulfilled and truly educated, they reasoned, then he needs the arts. Even their rhetoric sounded right:

> The modern approach to art education . . . provides a more flexible program which allows each child to grow as an individual, provides opportunities for each child to satisfy his creative impulses, develops sensitivity to the beauty in art products which he makes and observes, and enriches his living through the cultivation of skills and understandings. The modern art program is concerned with making art functional and meaningful to children, with enlisting the aid of persons in the local community who have special competencies in art, with making art an integral part of the total school program, and with extending art beyond the school into the life of the home, the community, and the state.[1]

As usual, good intentions were not enough.

Man was not fulfilled by the arts; he was filled with them.

Instead of making the arts a part of life, the institution set them apart from life.

Instead of the arts pervading the school, they were dismantled by the institution into rudimentary skills to be taught occasionally in measured doses. The arts became mere appendages to the graded curriculum.

And the rhetoric never said what the arts are really all about.

1. William B. Ragan, *Modern Elementary Curriculum* (New York: The Dryden Press, Inc., 1953).

90

First of all, they are for everybody—not just children. They are how people express themselves, the means by which they mold themselves. Feelings are shown in a finger painting, a clay sculpture, a dance.

Through the arts we make things, we build, plan, and design; we think great thoughts through simple materials. To gain self-confidence, to sense one's own competence is to make something one can take pride in because he knows it is his best.

Finally, the arts enable a person to feel he is one with all of the world's beautiful things. Because he feels that way, he makes his contribution to the beauty he finds, and rejects that which is ugly.

Then he does not need to be informed by Genesis that he was created in God's image. Because, like God, he has labored mightily to make something beautiful. And, behold, he *knows* that it is very good.

An art educator has said the schools believe that students of almost any age have the ability to produce something which for them is new, better, or unique when compared with their previous performances.

But creativity cannot be taught, it only can be stifled. The school tried to teach it. Skills in art, music, and writing must be exercised as an individual chooses if he is going to make something that he knows—and feels—is good. But for the school, it is often a sufficient end in itself if the skills are learned tolerably well.

Learned well enough to receive a passing mark.

Learned well enough to draw a poster announcing a litter drive or a pep rally, and warning peers to "walk on the green and not in between."

Learned well enough to join the marching band that plays the martial music that spurs on the football gladiators.

Learned well enough so that one's watercolor or ink sketch can hang with fifty other watercolors or ink sketches on a corridor wall.

Learned well enough so that one can sing before an audience just before Christmas and along about May.

Learned well enough so that one's composition can be corrected and marked for grammar, spelling, punctuation, and content.

The institution is a Philistine that grinds down teachers so that they not only demand little from their students, but demand little of themselves.

The distance between the pedagogues' good intentions and the mediocre practice compelled by the institution is no more than a few pages in the book *Children and Their Art* by Charles D. Gaitskell.[2] In chapter one, Gaitskell talks of art education nourishing creativity, preparing worthy citizens, and encouraging good taste. But in the very next chapter he says it can all happen at the hands of any pedant.

> The problems in teaching art, including classroom management and control, discipline, presentation of lessons, assistance of pupils, and appraisal of the success of the program are, broadly speaking, not distinct from the general school program.
>
> Art, like any other subject, of course, contains a certain content and requires of the teacher some specific knowledge and skills. A knowledge of pictorial composition and of other forms of design, an acquaintance with some professional art production, and some ability to use such media as paint, wood, or clay are required.
>
> However, the insights demanded of an art teacher in an elementary school are no more exacting than for any other subject. One may assert, therefore, that any proficient teacher in an elementary school may be a capable teacher of art.

Shakespeare said "the man that hath no music in himself" is not to be trusted, and "the motions of his spirit are dull as night."

But how deadly dull music can become when petrified in a school curriculum. A music education text[3] takes ten pages to tell the music teacher what to teach children at each stage of their physical and emotional growth. These are examples:

- When at age seven children are losing their first teeth but doing better at eye-hand coordination, it is time for "more skillful employment of percussion instruments, song bells, and piano in simple ways."

2. Charles D. Gaitskell, *Children and Their Art* (New York: Harcourt Brace Jovanovitch, Inc., 1958).

3. Robert Evans Nye and Vernice Trousdale Nye, *Music in the Elementary School* (Englewood Cliffs, N.J.: Prentice-Hall, Inc., 1957).

- The lungs and the digestive and circulatory systems are nearly fully developed at age nine, so "instruction on some band and orchestral instruments may begin."

- At age ten and eleven, children are on the verge of rapid physical growth. The implications for teaching music are to "enlarge upon the activities listed for the [nine-year-olds] with the following additions: activities such as the grand march and floor patterns aid in overcoming awkwardness; rhythmic activities planned to improve coordination; study, appreciation, and skill in the basic steps of the polka, schottische, and the square dance; social dance steps for the [all-year-olds]."

The school has professed that the arts—and these include, of course, more than art, music, and writing—are important to the child. But the institution gives ample indication that it considers the arts to be relatively unimportant, and the very creative person to be a little weird.

The school has convinced parents that marks on the report card and comments of the teacher at the parent-teacher conference are true indicators of how well their child is doing in the subjects that count. But as with physical education and health, the typical elementary-school report card gives no mark for the arts, and the teacher frequently does not comment on the child's work in art and music. If there is an art or music teacher, the parent probably will never meet them.

The school typically assumes that the fulfilled and well-educated man has learned all he needs to learn about art and music by the time he leaves the eighth grade. After that, the subjects become electives or club activities, and the institution makes it difficult for many students to enroll in them because of the burden of courses deemed necessary to college or a good job.

Creative writing has been separated from all other writing called composition. The child learns quickly, therefore, that most of what he writes in school is expected to be noncreative and is certainly not intended to bring him any more joy than an "A" or a "well done" from the teacher.

The school and the community offer few rewards and scant praise for those who reach for the highest edges of creativity in art, music, and writing.

The school does not encourage or expect students to know real greatness on the stage. At best, the theater arts are seen as an extracurricular club activity; at worst, plays are produced to raise money for the class treasury. After all, every graduating class is expected to give something back to the alma mater—like a scoreboard that lights up or shrubbery.

Dance as a creative expression is pretty much restricted to a piece of the physical education program only for girls in the high school. But even though modern dance forms can be tremendously exhilarating for participants, girls sometimes are made to feel that the activity is just a break from calisthenics, basketball, or volleyball.

Making things out of wood, metal, and leather typically are considered part of the industrial arts by the school, and industrial arts are traditionally thought of by school leaders as appendages designed mainly for those who can't or won't go to college.

Both the school and the community tend to look suspiciously at the exceptionally creative person in the arts. He brings to their mind all of the ancient, terrible stereotypes—homosexual, alcoholic, drug addict, psychopath.

While trying to make the arts come alive in the school, the pedagogues nearly have smothered them. While installing the arts into the school's rather humdrum routine, the institution took them away from the American people.

An article in the September 1970 issue of *Nation's Schools*[4] said: "The stress in arts courses on performance and 'how to do it'— rather than on underlying concepts, experiences, and emotions which could help students understand themselves, their environment, and the continuity of history—has helped to reinforce the isolation of the arts."

Man needs the arts every day, all day. Through them he can dredge out of his soul what is most deeply felt and perceived and

4. "Curriculum Planning," *Nation's Schools* 86, no. 3 (September 1970).

ennoble it in song, granite, oils, carefully chosen words and meter, body movement, or on celluloid.

But the school has institutionalized the arts; set it aside to be taught just before recess or just after lunch, in third and fifth periods only, from 9:10 to 9:50 A.M. every other day, after school from 3:30 P.M. until the club adviser goes home.

Through the arts, Man can delight in what is most beautiful in his world and remind himself of what is most ugly. But the arts as taught and tolerated in the school lead children toward no such lofty and necessary aims.

Gaitskell in his book admits that until the early fifties it did not occur to the schools that through art, Americans might do something about their taste.

"In 1934," Gaitskell wrote,

> Dewey asked the question, "Why is the architecture of our cities so unworthy of a fine civilization? It is not from lack of materials nor lack of technical capacity . . . yet it is not merely slums but the apartments of the well-to-do that are aesthetically repellent."
>
> Statements such as these offered a challenge to education, for such condemnations referred not to artists but to the mass of the people who were the product of public schools. The inference could be made, and indeed was made, that the program of art education was not effective in developing people with the ability to discriminate good design from bad. As a result, art educators have comparatively recently begun to give serious consideration to methods of developing taste.

But the school is not equal to such a task. How can it be? Drawing a poster that implores Americans to keep America beautiful will not help make it beautiful as much as an expression of beauty in a painting and a sonnet that the artist and the poet *know* are beautiful because, behold, they can see that they are very good.

We will not find the taste old Dewey was looking for in our architecture until the school and the larger community pay as much homage to the creative soul as they do to the clever mind that can figure how to make a bundle on a construction job or save a bundle by cutting corners.

The nation that amassed the most power and the most wealth in the last twenty centuries of civilization might be in danger of fading from the scene without making major contributions in the arts and general culture that will be worth remembering and revering.

Many still offer thanks to the ancient Greeks for what they accomplished in the arts and passed on to posterity. But generations of Americans may only be damned in the future for mass producing the gasoline combustible engine and city architecture that cluttered the urban scene, for burying garbage in the earth and hauling excrement out to sea, for putting up nearly indestructible signs that light up and say "Smoke," "Drink," "Spray," or "Eat."

The emasculation of the arts in the graded and appended school has not only made it nearly impossible for children to experience the rapture of creation and to contribute to the beauty of the earth, it has made it nearly impossible for what is good, or struggling to be good, in our culture to get inside the school.

Jazz—created in the souls of our black people—is an American export more treasured than Ford Galaxies, Boeing 707s, and Bic ball-point pens. The late Louis Armstrong put jazz in his trumpet and hauled it to Europe and Africa, played it for England's king and a tribal chief in Ghana. But neither he nor anyone else ever had much success at getting jazz past the closed doors of the American public school's music room.

Indeed, the best one prominent music educator[5] could say about jazz when it was at its zenith in its native land was that "a work in the jazz idiom (whatever that may be), does not, perhaps, express and convey the profoundest and most significant of human emotions, but the idea that its effective content is essentially demoralizing and debasing will hardly bear analysis."

In days of old, the culture was transmitted frequently through music. Ancient history and slightly old news of the changing world were broadcast by wandering troubadours. Once more, such a time is at hand. Today's newest generation finds it easier to communicate its deepest emotions and best thoughts to the accom-

5. James L. Marsell, *Music in American Schools* (Morristown, N.J.: Silver Burdett Co., 1943).

paniment of a guitar. Listen to these lyrics composed by a high school student:

- "Miss Smith comes in and says, 'Hello. Won't you step into my office?' She sits in her chair and says I'm failing. And for lack of better words, I say, 'Gee Whiz!' She says, 'You'd better get on top of that Spanish. If you do your homework, you'll find—saints be praised! saints be praised! —that you'll pass Spanish and life will be roses and wine.' I say, 'Really, Miss Smith? I didn't know that homework was the key to life, that if everyone did their homework there would be no riots, no strife.' "

- (To the tune of "America the Beautiful") "O Hideous, for crowded skies; the airplane's seen to this. Where once were mountain majesties, now ugly highways twist! America, America, I shed my tears for thee. Don't crown thy mess with more distress. Why is it you can't see?

  "O Hideous for visions grim that see beyond the years thine black and filthy cities rot; proud eyes are filled with tears! America, America, I shed my tears for thee. Don't crown thy mess with more distress. Why is it you can't see?"

This is how the kids say their piece. But when a high school junior was asked if he ever heard any of today's folk music in school, he replied, "No, I haven't heard *any* music in school, except the band."

Not only does the institution virtually ignore the creative and communicative music on the tongues of America's youths, it hardly ever acknowledges the guitar as an instrument. Countless boys and girls in their early teens are composing on the guitar, saying something that comes up from deep inside, but the school pays little heed. After all, can they march on Saturday afternoons in autumn?

Not long ago, school board members of an East Coast district spent a day visiting the district's high school to find out what students had to say about education as it is and education as it might be.

"There is a stereotype of a student," one boy told a board member in his classroom.

> The school figures there are abilities that a student is *supposed* to have. If he doesn't have these abilities, he doesn't measure up.
>
> But maybe students have other abilities. For instance, I make films after school, but the administration and the faculty don't care because filmmaking is not an accepted ability.

In another high school, two boys became quite excited over their idea to make a film and submit it as their term paper in English. Because the project worked out so well, the school decided to purchase a limited amount of filmmaking equipment for the following year. But the equipment is for a new club that meets once a week after school. Once more the schedule has killed enthusiasm.

The students who had shown the school system that filmmaking is a worthwhile art too, had done some of their shooting in New York City. One wonders how members of the new club will get to do much shooting in the city or anywhere else remote from the school during an hour or two after school.

When students at a high school in Pennsylvania were given the freedom to conceive their own mini courses to fill free periods during the day, they decided mostly on arts and crafts—leatherwork, macramé, etc.

Most of these students were headed for college, so few of them had been able to elect an art course in the high school. But if they had enrolled in a traditional art course, they would have had little or no opportunity to engage in the kind of work they really wanted to do.

We said earlier that the school doesn't regard the arts too highly and is not concerned that only a few students are ever able to experience the inner warmth that comes from creating something that the creator knows is very good.

Because the institution considers the arts as subjects to be taught and not as ways to life's most joyful experiences, teachers generally are called upon to hold students accountable for only the most minimal standards. Providing the kids do what they're told, show some effort, and don't misuse or wantonly destroy materials, they can expect compliments and satisfactory marks from the teachers.

Sometimes—not very often—a teacher will act as though he knows the students will receive no satisfaction from their creations unless they are confident that what they have done is good—their best. Such rewards are so much greater than high marks and pats on the back that a comparison of their value is impossible.

We visited a junior high school in a city ghetto, but it could have been Anyplace, U.S.A. Most of the arts teachers did what they were asked and paid to do—show kids what to do and hope they could do it without being too messy and without hurting themselves or others.

In the shops there were examples of woodwork, clay casting, leather tooling, and metalwork that could be found in the shops of almost every junior and senior high school in the country. The students' creations were crude and carelessly done. There was a joint where the joined parts didn't really fit; there was a soldering job where the solder had overflowed; there were file scratches that badly marred a finished surface; there were patches of putty everywhere.

The students displayed their work perfunctorily, reticently, and without enthusiasm. Although it was expected that visitors would say a few kind words about the boys' work, it was obvious that the students took little heart from such comments as "Well, this certainly shows effort" and "Been working hard, haven't you?" They took no satisfaction from the comments because they *knew* their work was inferior. There had been no joy of creation.

In one shop, however, a remarkable teacher held forth. The students excitedly pushed each other in an effort to be the first, or at least the second one, to show off his work. There were hand-tooled wooden cabinets that equaled anything found in better furniture stores, leather belts on a par with anything produced by master craftsmen, and jewelry the boys' mothers would wear proudly, not because their sons made it but because it looked like quality. Everything was done well and with good taste by these children from the slums.

We lavished deserved praise and stopped to talk to the teacher.

He was a serious person—intense and demanding; he was not the stereotype of the all-American teacher with bright smile and friendly word. We asked him why his students' work was so extraordinary, why they could do what most kids in the country their age and older could not do and did not do.

He explained, to the accompaniment of his students' laughter and shouts of "Yea, man!" and "Right on!" that he did not expect or accept shoddy work. "If you are going to sandpaper something, you do it until it's smooth; if you cut metal, you cut it with care; if you solder, you wind up with a clean joint. A person can't take satisfaction from something he doesn't think is very good. To do a good piece of work, you have to work hard. What I demand must be at the edge of the boys' own ideas of what is good. I would rather stretch them than let them down."

In school after school across America there are children who take no satisfaction and have no reason to feel pride in their sandpapering, soldering, sculpting, painting, writing, blowing a horn, playing the piano, or photography. They practice the skills the teacher has taught, but feel too little and know almost no goodness.

Fortunately, there are some teachers like the shop man we just introduced. He beat the system. His unique drive, insights, and fortitude enabled his students to know the craftsman's joy. There are such teachers in a few classrooms who, by their courageous uniqueness, transcend the mediocrity engineered by the institution.

The institution doesn't care because the pedagogues only said that the arts should be added to the curriculum; they didn't say the arts were the stuff that made possible a quality of life, a joy in living.

The article in *Nation's Schools* quoted Alfred North Whitehead as saying forty years ago that if education were separated from life, it would be a fatal disconnection. The article continued:

> In spite of the warnings of Whitehead and many others, nowhere has that "fatal disconnection" been more obvious than in art education—an area which has seldom been woven into the fabric of the general curriculum. Art education has been, and continues to be, regared as a "frill," easily discarded when budgets must be cut.

The article thought that perhaps the most promising way to reconnect life and the arts would be to try a new "interdisciplinary or humanities approach to art education."

While there is no question that the arts should be related to the other subjects of the curriculum and should be used as a means of communication in all subjects, the suggestion does not go far enough.

The "interdisciplinary or humanities approach" might insure that the arts would be used more widely and wisely, but it does not seem to us that the linkage of teachers of the arts with teachers of other subjects will provide that vital link between life and the arts.

We submit that the arts, if they are to become truly central in people's lives, must be center stage in the community. We suggest, therefore, that a Community Arts Center be one of the new public institutions under the governance of our Education Assembly and under the strict control of its own board of elected parents and community residents.

We would remove the present instruction in the arts from the school. But in so doing, we would put more of the arts into the school. The article in *Nation's Schools* partially explains the paradox.

The arts have been considered as appendages to the curriculum, as collections of elementary skills to be taught formally and occasionally.

Now, in the school itself, and aside from the Community Arts Center, the arts consistently would be used by students to communicate. And we are talking of uses that far exceed the mass construction of sugar-cube castles and papier-mâché volcanoes and the mass drawing of pictures of Thanksgiving turkeys and Easter rabbits.

The magazine article tells of an undertaking in a Salt Lake City school: "In one sample unit, students studied the Greek period, wrote a Greek play using a modern theme, designed sets, made costumes, composed their own music, constructed their own musical instruments, and filmed the performance." If quality was demanded and quality given, then it's the kind of use of the arts we are talking about in the school.

Creative writing and composition writing would not be two different subjects, and writing of any kind would not be the sole means of expressing ideas and feelings. Here's what we mean.

- A boy speaks of the problems of the ecology through a song he composed himself and accompanies on the guitar.
- A girl discusses the loneliness of youth through a series of poignant 8½-by-11 photographs of friends and strangers in different settings.
- A boy describes the Old West using selected paintings by Remington, some charcoal sketches of his own, slides from a trip with his family, and songs played on a harmonica.
- A group of students spends months filming the gypsy moth, first in its caterpillar stage as it devours oak leaves, then building its cocoon, and finally emerging as a moth.
- Boys and girls choreograph their interpretation of the Bill of Rights and compose the music for the dance.
- A young boy and girl are commissioned by a committee of fellow students to sculpt busts of Martin Luther King and Robert Kennedy for a special program on race relations being planned by the committee.
- Three boys design and draw to scale the municipal park they have conceived.
- A group of students builds a model for a new public housing unit that would be attractive and inspiring to the inhabitants as well as functional.

All of these communications through the arts would be directly related to learning in the school. And their inspiration would be our Community Arts Center—where the eighty-five-year-old would be as welcome as the five-year-old, where the joy of creating would be commonplace, and the teaching of skills as an end in itself would not exist at all.

The Community Arts Center is a perfect example of our philosophy about education. We have spoken before of the difference between our proposed Education Assembly and the present board of education. One of the most critical differences is this: today's board of education is concerned with governing and administering a school or a system of schools designed exclusively for children in twelve grades.

While they are in school, the children are nearly segregated from all adults who are not properly labeled faculty, staff, or paraprofessionals. This exclusionary behavior on the part of the institution is an unintentional, but nevertheless significant, cause of the unhealthy and unnatural gap between persons of different ages.

The adults, if they are allowed in the school at all, must come at night. And usually they must pay a fee to take a course. Although the same board of education has jurisdiction over the adult school, there is hardly any relation between the school for children during the day and the school for adults at night.

Our Education Assembly would not administer schools; it would be concerned with education in the community. Being thus concerned, the assembly would want to make education available to all members of the community. The Family Health Center would be one expression of this philosophy, and the Community Arts Center is another. The Education Assembly is not wedded to schools as the only means of education and the end of education.

The center would be a place where people work in the arts, not come to watch others work, although there would be a time for watching. But Americans are too much engaged in watching others perform in the arts, going to museums to look at what others brought forth out of the pain and joy of their creation, reading what others have written, singing and playing songs others have composed, watching others dance and act, marveling at others' contributions in architecture. Looking is not enough.

So, the center would be mostly a place for doing. And what things there would be to do!

- There would be studios for painting, sculpting, and playing musical instruments.
- There would be places to design and fashion clothes, to

learn upholstering, to master the art of interior decoration, to design houses and neighborhoods.

- There would be stages to produce Shakespeare and an original play by Cynthia Jones (apartment 15A in the Metropolitan Housing Center). Sometimes plays would be staged for free and sometimes for money.

- On the same stages, modern dance and ballet would hold forth. And the center would search out the talented boy who could block out the complicated movements for a big dance number in an upcoming musical production.

- In a big room, a symphony orchestra would rehearse works by Beethoven, Bernstein, and Blessington—a local church organist who retired after forty years' service. In another room, a rock band would be composing and playing songs, a few of which would be recorded by a staff headed during the day by three teenage boys and at night by an executive with a record company. In other rooms, there would be a concert band, maybe a string quartet.

- There would be shops for creating things out of wood, metal, styrofoam, clay, and soap. There would be a place to work in leather, macrame, lapidary, crewel, and needle-point.

- There would be a place to learn about photography and a place to develop and print, but most of the picture-taking would go on out in the community. There would be studios where films are made and rooms to edit films taken in a slum, on a river, in a train, inside a jail, of babies and old people, of blacks and Poles, of animals and fountains, of towering buildings and budding flowers— and closeups of us.

- Down the hall would be studios for producing television shows to be beamed into shut-ins' rooms where sick students and the home-bound elderly could learn and enjoy, into a public hospital to entertain and inform patients, into homes to bring important ideas to the attention of new mothers.

The work of the Community Arts Center would flow from the community and back into it, raising the quality of living to a level never before experienced in any community of these United States.

Today, in a town of 15,000 to 25,000 or in urban neighborhoods of like size, it is not uncommon to find one school marching band, a school choir and small church choirs, one small theater group, a couple of private art and music teachers, and not much else. We envision such a community having many varied musical groups, several theater groups, and people of all ages engaging in the other arts.

The place would be alive with the sounds of music—and the sounds, sights, smells, and feels of all of the other art forms.

The people's involvement in the arts would prompt them to look for beauty in themselves and others, in the homes they buy and remodel, in the furniture and wallpaper they select, in the public buildings they sanction, on Main Street and along the highway, in the wilderness of the country and in the biggest cities of the land, in the state and national capitals, on the theater screen and stage, on the television tube, between hard covers and paperbacks, on records and in cassettes—everywhere.

Americans would create a taste for good things as they create good things themselves. The shabby and the shoddy would be rejected by a community of craftsmen and artists.

The Community Arts Center would be a place where children would go not as a class, or an assignment, but because participation in the arts would be their choice. A child might spend half a day there every day for a week, or two hours one week and five the next; maybe one hour in the morning and two hours at night. And mothers, fathers, uncles, aunts, grandparents, policemen, physicists, storekeepers, stock brokers, bus drivers, and dentists would schedule themselves on the same basis.

The center staff would consist mainly of persons who practice the arts; some would work full time for experience and some would work part time for pay. The teachers of the arts taken out of the school would be employed according to their ability. A teacher who has been satisfied with routinely and dully teaching the rudi-

mentary arts skills might find himself to be a student in the center
before he can be a teacher in the center.

The performing artists and professional craftsmen of the community, now excluded by antiquated certification rules and repelled
by the institution's deadly dullness, would be attracted and invited to join in the great goings-on.

The Community Arts Center would share the same roof with a
community museum and library.

The museum would be an ever-revolving mirror of the community as it was, as it is, and as it might be. There would be such
displays as a mastodon's bones unearthed by a team composed of
archeologists and local children, an exhibit of oils painted by
persons aged ten to eighty, a large scale model showing how the industrial area could be landscaped in the future to give it maximum
human quality, samples of local flora and fauna, and an exhibit of
colonial style furniture handcrafted in the arts center. And on and
on. (Including the culinary arts of the practicing gourmets?)

The work of the arts center, the exhibits in the museum, and the
contents of the library would be mobile insofar as possible. A play
would be performed at the hospital and macramé would be taught
to the residents of the nursing home; photography would be introduced and continued in the jail; books, records, and tapes would
go regularly to the orphanage.

And the center and museum would serve the community as did
students from the Parsons School of Design during the winter and
spring of 1971. They redecorated Ward 16 in Brooklyn State
Hospital, a crowded facility for alcoholics and schizophrenics. *The
New York Times* (July 17, 1971) quoted a recent graduate of the
school as saying: "When we first came here, the furniture was placed
against the walls and all we could see was a line of patients sitting
in these chairs not doing anything at all." The walls were an institutional green, most of the furniture was in disrepair, and everything was dirty.

The students changed it all, involving some of the patients in
the renovation. Speaking of the effect of the students' effort, Dr.
Edward Perrotti, a psychiatrist and hospital administrator, said

it "was definitely good for the patients. When the patients become interested in their surroundings, this in itself is therapeutic."

In America today, the public and school libraries work well together on paper but hardly at all in fact. We would combine school and public libraries into exciting learning centers directly related to the Community Arts Centers.

Beauty, of course, would have to begin with the arts center and the associated museum and library. These places must be as inviting in their physical appearance as they are in their programs on the inside.

In many schools today, the library is not a good place to go. Listen to high school students in an upper middle-class community talk about their school library:

- "The librarians are too restrictive and too severe. I don't want to go there any more."
- "The library is only open for an hour after school."
- "Nobody wants to go there unless they have to be there."
- "If you ask a friend for help in finding a book, you get kicked out for talking."

In many schools, students can go to the library only when their class goes, only on special assignment, or only during study hall. And many librarians who know better are compelled by the institution's image of libraries as morgues for dead books to be concerned more with keeping children quiet than keeping students profitably occupied with materials they want and need.

There have been some welcome developments in libraries in recent years—the addition of such things as microfilm-viewing machines, tape recorders, cassette and record players, film and slide viewers, and collections of art prints that may be checked out like books.

But those changes perhaps have come faster than the change needed to transform libraries from cold, unfriendly, and overly regimented places where "nobody wants to go" to warm, friendly, and helpful places where everybody wants to go—and does.

Not many libraries provide places where groups can gather to discuss or debate, sending members out occasionally to get books and other materials to substantiate points and positions. Our combined public and school library would have such private, sound-proofed rooms.

Record collections would include many albums and singles made by modern groups, as well as records representing all other varieties of music and taped recordings of the events of our times.

The library, like the arts center and the museum, would be open all day every day and until late at night—and for oldsters as well as youngsters.

The schools have been guilty of considering elderly residents enemies of education. They assume that old people have no interest in the schools and are concerned only that the education tax gets no more of their fixed incomes.

We believe that the extended-hand policy of our institutions would go a long way toward alleviating the alienation between schools and older residents of the community. Consider the feeling a retired couple might have toward education if man and wife were able to find all manner of things of interest to do at the arts center and no longer had to wait to take up lapidary and woodworking until they left town for a segregated community of senior citizens.

And would an older citizen have the same misunderstandings about young people (and vice versa) if he had an easel next to a boy with long hair, if he wrote a play with children of all ages, if he could show a twelve-year-old how to take better photographs of birds?

The Community Arts Center, the museum, and the library would be beautiful places where beauty would be made and seen and felt.

The nation's leaders have urged us to make America beautiful. But as a people we are capable of completing the task only if we make the arts central to our lives and become participants and not merely observers.

We will have to praise and hold in high esteem musicians, sculptors, playwrights, and poets. Our "best people" need to include craftsmen, and our heroes need to include artists.

Let it begin with the Community Arts Center.

Six

Youths Apprenticed to Their Future

BEGINNING IN THE LATE NINETEENTH CENTURY, when it became another appendage to America's public schools, vocational education has been the track into a world of work where everybody is supposed to have dirty fingernails and wear sweat-stained blue collars.

Vocational education from its inception was seen as something different from *real* education. The former was intended to enable some students to get and hold jobs as trained craftsmen. The latter was an intellectual exercise intended to enable the other students to get into college.

Vocational education was born at a time when technology was changing forever the American Way of Life, and the nation's booming industries looked to the schools to help satisfy their voracious appetite for skilled workers. It also was a time when people in foreign lands who dreamed dreams sailed in great numbers to our shores so that their dreams might come true. And the nation asked the schools to find a way to get the immigrants and their children into the labor market.

The schools saw unclearly then that persons whose jobs required them to have clean hands and starched white collars (and perhaps a framed sheepskin) were in business and the professions, not the world of work. The schools' incredible double vision, a continuing affliction, has shortchanged millions of children. College preparation became an elitist goal for all but the unfortunates who had to be trained to work.

109

Vocational education in the public schools was given a shot in the arm in 1917, when the Smith-Hughes Act authorized the first injections of federal money "to provide for cooperation with the states in promotion of . . . education in agriculture and the trades and industries."

But the Smith-Hughes Act also proved to be a kick in the head. It put the Congress of the United States on record as saying that the schools' faulty vision of the world of work was just right. It officially defined that world as one containing only farmers, factory hands, and seamstresses.

Doctors, lawyers, and insurance executives were obviously excluded because they were in another world—a world where work was not even thought of as work. One simply went to the office.

Children either elected vocational education as defined and supported by the federal government (with matching funds from the state), or they were switched onto the vocational track by school officials who said they knew what was best; in either case, they found themselves effectively cut off from children destined for bigger and better things in business and the professions via college.

The tracks ran separately even under the same roof. But when vocational education students—"vokes"—were sent off to a school intended only for them, it meant there never would be a chance that the tracks might intersect.

The Smith-Hughes Act also firmly implanted vocational education in a collection of shops, and the vokes had to take so many shop hours a week if they were to be eligible for the benefits of the federally funded program. It is a rut plowed so deep that massive efforts in recent years to get vocational education out of it have met with scant success.

When it got started, vocational education was caught between two very strong and competing strands in the fabric of American society. On the one hand was the Protestant ethic which said that hard work is good for the soul. Although it was mostly preached by persons who did not have to do the hard work, the people for whom the sermon was intended—the laborers in the fields and factories—might take satisfaction in their work twelve hours a day, six days a week.

On the other hand, there was the aristocratic tradition insisting that manual labor is a bad thing, that it is far better to be one of the lilies than one of the hands in the field. It is this piece of our heritage that makes us thank God for Fridays, that makes us overstay our coffee breaks, and prompts us to retire from our job at the earliest opportunity.

The appendage called vocational education was good at satisfying the Protestant ethic. If you could get closer to God by working a plow, a lathe, or a sewing machine, then the Smith-Hughes Act was the stairway to Paradise.

But vocational education was—and still is—in disharmony with the aristocratic tradition. Anybody who wanted the good American life that only money and a college degree could buy wanted no part of a program with a virtual guarantee that big money, status, and a college degree were not at the end of the track.

The fact that in the early 1970s there are a lot of men in blue collars taking home a fatter paycheck then many of their brothers in white (or striped and polka-dot) collars has not diluted the influence of the aristocratic tradition. It only means that today's snobbery is as outdated as much of the vocational education curriculum.

No matter how vocational education has expanded its offerings and no matter how hard it has promoted a first-class image among educators in charge of the college-bound track and among the general public, it still bends under the burden of second-class status.

The National Advisory Council on Vocational Education says: "At the very heart of our problem is a national attitude that says vocational education is designed for somebody else's children. This attitude is shared by businessmen, labor leaders, administrators, teachers, parents, and students . . ."

The academicians predominate in public education and dominate the news media. Consequently, the National Advisory Council complains, they have convinced the American people that the only good education is the kind that culminates in a bachelor's, master's, or—best of all—a doctoral degree.

Grant Venn, former Associate Commissioner for Adult, Vocational, and Library Programs in the United States Office of Education, has described vocational education's image problem in the book *Man, Education, and Manpower*.[1] "Its students too often are the dropouts or castoffs of the academic curriculum. Its teachers . . . enjoy relatively low status within the teaching profession in many states. Its buildings are often the oldest, its facilities the poorest . . . Its subject matter suffers from the general debasement of manual and blue-collar occupations in contemporary social values.

"The low repute of the program is harmful in many ways; good students shy away, teachers are difficult to recruit, industry remains standoffish, other educators show little interest, and money is difficult to come by."

Vocational education began by preparing kids for an extremely limited world of work, which the middle and upper classes immediately disdained and which aspiring members of the working class also came to resent. And nothing that has happened since the Smith-Hughes Act—including more recent and more extensive federal legislation—has done much to wipe away the early stigma.

- In the early part of 1971, a board of education in an affluent suburb acted embarrassed because it had to admit that it was contemplating a room for instruction in beauty culture in the plans for an expanded high school.
- A regional vocational high school offering a wide variety of courses in modern and attractive buildings has difficulty in meeting its enrollment quota in an area with a population approaching 1 million.
- United States Commissioner of Education Sidney P. Marland, Jr., felt compelled to confess before an audience composed of the nation's secondary-school principals: "You, like me, have been preoccupied most of the time with college entrance expectations. The vocational education teachers and administrators have been either scorned or condemned and we have been silent."
- The visitor walks into a vocational education shop—and

1. Grant Venn, *Man, Education, and Manpower* (Washington, D.C.: American Association of School Administrators, 1970).

it can be anywhere in the country—where he finds kids unengaged, uninterested, and unenthusiastic. Instead of being resented as an intruder, the visitor is viewed only as a routine interruption in an excruciatingly routine day. The students know what the visitor knows: they don't have what it takes to go to college and be in big business or the professions; they are second-class citizens.

- A high school junior has never known or heard of a student who was enrolled in Distributive Education (where students work part time, principally in retail stores). Moreover, in three years he has never heard of his school's Distributive Education program.

- A girl just turned fifteen is written up in *The New York Times* because she already has become a professional designer of clothes. But across the United States girls who prefer designing and making clothes—and are good at it —are considered by school officials, other students, and maybe even their parents to be a cut below girls who excel in science or are enrolled in honors classes in English lit.

As usual, a prime victim of institutional behavior is the teacher. The typical attitude of the academic institution toward vocational education is tolerance of what are considered deadly, dull courses leading to dead ends.

The vocational education teacher—wait a minute, we might as well call him by the label that he wears—the shop teacher comes to his position in the school either as a journeyman with perhaps ten years experience in his field, or as a graduate of a bachelor's degree program in industrial arts.

He hardly has had time to check out his equipment before he feels the pressure to be somebody he isn't, to look like a teacher of almost anything but what he is a teacher of. Nothing has to be said and nothing has to be put in writing, but the institution's message is explicit: "If you want to get along in this school, if you want to be accepted (at least as much as is your due considering your credentials), you have to behave like a *real* teacher."

A "real teacher," of course, is one that instructs students in algebra I, or Spanish III, or modern European history, or some other respectable academic subject.

The shop teacher feels self-conscious, embarrassed at being what he is. So, he begins to copy, or mimic, the pedagogical methods used by the academic teachers who are his social superiors, not his peers. Instead of relying upon the demonstration techniques used since time began between master craftsman and apprentice, he lectures: he talks and talks and talks. And he looks far and wide for books and manuals from which his students can learn how to do something they have not been given a chance to do. He apes all the worst techniques employed by the rest of the faculty.

To find out if his students know how to operate a lathe safely, the shop teacher asks them to take a paper-and-pencil test where they must write down "four precautions the lathe operator should take if he is going to operate his equipment safely and efficiently."

Instead of observing the student as he employs different kinds of chisels, the teacher gives the student paper and pencil and asks him to "name three different kinds of chisels and how they are used in the shop." Or the shop teacher demands a written explanation of how to set up a jig, rather than watching as the student sets up a jig.

We have visited a vocational school where a conventional classroom has been attached to the bake shop so that the master baker doesn't forget he's still in a situation where he must demonstrate to outsiders that *even* an instructor in baking has a little of the academician in him.

The absurdity of the master baker's pretense is evidenced by the fact that the students who really know how to decorate a wedding cake or make an almond Danish ring are hardly ever found in the classroom. That is mainly reserved for kids who don't know what they're doing in the bake shop and for the troublemakers.

Tragically, the abused emulates the abuser. And the shop teacher trying to behave like, and gain the acceptance of, the academic teachers requires his students to perform in ways that they are in vocational education to avoid. Since many students are counseled into vocational courses because the academicians have decided they can't make the grade in their courses, it is grossly stupid to subject these students to the same teaching and learning practices that they could not, or would not, accept before. Trying to transform skills into the abstract world of written and spoken words is bad teaching that leads to bad learning.

The intention of the vocational education program—whether it be under the same roof with the academic program or in another building in another part of town—has been to prepare students for a world of work that really existed and really needed them.

But the truth is the facilities of the vocational education program often have been expensive antiques in the field—early versions of equipment that have been revised or replaced several times since.

And it is the truth that much of what has been taught in the vocational shop has been unrelated to the skills then in use by practitioners in that vocation. Furthermore, it is the truth that vocational education has taken in relatively few of those who might have profited from some exposure to its offerings, and has graduated and placed in jobs not enough of those who were enrolled.

We visited a machine shop in an academic—or comprehensive—high school which gave every outward apearance of being the perfect place for preparing students for jobs in machine shops in the real world of work. The room was huge—about 4,000 square feet, with an 18-foot ceiling that featured overhead tracks for moving heavy loads. On the reinforced concrete floor there were highly polished lathes, milling machines, cutters, and other pieces of equipment.

About half of the machines were federal surplus, but the school district had purchased the remainder of the equipment. The total value of the shop and its equipment was a quarter of a million dollars, of which $100,000 was the local capital investment.

We examined the shop records for the last five years and discovered that only forty-five students had graduated from the instruction offered in that expensive shop during the period—*nine students a year*. The records also showed that approximately eighteen students typically began the instruction in their sophomore year. So, the dropout rate was 50 percent over a two- or three-year period.

The costs of instruction were phenomenal—$2,000 per student. That figure, of course, does not include the cost of instructing the student in the other subjects in which he was enrolled. The instructor was being paid $11,000 a year, so each of the nine students in the graduating class shared more than $1,200 of that expense.

The real shock came when we checked with the largest machine shop in the city to find out how many of the graduates from the school's program were hired there. The shop not only had never employed a graduate of the program, the men who ran the business didn't even know the school was training students in the field.

When acquainted with the facts, the vice-president for personnel was ready to guarantee that his shop, which employed more than 300 persons, would hire from three to five of the school's most accomplished graduates every year.

The shop teacher, who had not earned his livelihood at the trade for fifteen years, discovered at the machine shop that some of the techniques he was still teaching were now archaic. He immediately corrected what he and his students were doing wrong.

This is a case where everything about a school's major offering in vocational education had an unreal quality and had completely lost touch with the very world of work for which it was preparing students.

We wish the machine shop were an exception, but it is more the rule. The courses, the techniques, the equipmnt, the teachers, and the students in vocational education are remote from the world of work because once again the institution has paid almost no heed to its good intentions.

The academic institution doesn't carry out its intentions primarily because it has regarded vocational education from the beginning as an appended program for that handful of students who always have been headaches to the "real" teachers. To some degree the vocational and technical high school also has failed to prepare all of its students for reality. And the reason, paradoxically, is probably because it has tried so hard and so long to be like the academic high school.

In advance of the drafting of the Vocational Education Act of 1963, a distinguished panel appointed by President Kennedy probed and studied vocational education in the country for a full year. In the end, the panel had to conclude that vocational education had been insensitive to economic and social change, to labor market demands, to the impact of change on job preparation, and to the increasingly varied vocational needs of the American people.

The indictment was made in the fall of 1962. It could be made today.

The 1963 legislation that the panel's report led to was designed to train students in a wide range of occupations and to provide on-the-job experience. The keynote was flexibility, and the law was committed to keeping open at all times the lines of communication between vocational education and vocations.

Four or five years later, the Advisory Council on Vocational Education reported that the Vocational Education Act of 1963 had not accomplished much of what it set out to do. The council did what any such body is expected to do; it blamed the failure on insufficient funds and called for another federal aid program. It got what it asked for in the form of 1968 amendments to the 1963 Act.

One of the federal government's special programs in vocational training was the Neighborhood Youth Corps, established in 1964. From then until mid-1968, the corps placed nearly 1.6 million young persons from low-income families, including many school dropouts, in some work situation.

Unfortunately, much of the placement was in make-work jobs in governmental agencies. The corps recruits in such a situation found they were neither trained for very much nor were they expected to do very much.

Probably the best that can be said for the Neighborhod Youth Corps during the period is that it took off the streets, at just the right time, a lot of unemployed youths who James B. Conant once labeled "social dynamite."

Perhaps the worst that can be said about the corps program was said by Grant Venn in his book:

> A recent in-depth study of 2,000 youths formerly enrolled in the NYC out-of-school program found that, on the average, this group did not have a significantly better employment situation than a con-

trol group of non-NYC enrollees, nor did they return to school in larger proportions.

The findings suggested that the program be bolstered with closer links between training and real jobs, more effective techniques for motivating return to school, and possibly more emphasis on remedial education.

For more than seventy years now the appended vocational education has been struggling without notable success. It began with an extremely limited vision of the world of work, was kept within those narrow limits by poorly conceived federal aid programs, and has had great difficulty seeing any more clearly despite almost ten years of more liberal and more expansive federal programs. It has required costly input for minimal output, and it has often been either incapable of recognizing the gap between what it was doing and reality, or unable to do anything to close the gap.

As if the English language were not already abundantly cluttered and utterly confused by acronyms, there are some vocational educators and government bureaucrats who now cryptically refer to the world of work as simply WOW.

Unfortunately, "Ugh!" is about the only appropriate response to much of what America's public schools have done and are doing to prepare kids for WOW.

In his speech on career education in January 1971 at the convention of the National Association of Secondary School Principals, United States Commissioner of Education Sidney P. Marland, Jr., pledged that reform of vocational education would be "one of a very few major emphases" during his administration.

We welcome the federal government's commitment. And we would offer as one worthy instrument of reform our proposed Career Education Center.

Again, we have taken an appendage to the public school that has not functioned well, transplanted it out of the school into a new setting, and then radically transformed it.

The center would primarily be concerned with seeing the world of work through 20/20 eyes. We would free it from the chronic blurred vision that has seen the world of work as excluding people who work at big jobs in big business, who work in the professions, and who have a degree after their name.

- We believe that the teen-ager who thinks he wants to be a lawyer should have early access to the world of work in that profession, as surely as the teen-ager who thinks he would like to repair cars should have a crack at work in a service station. Or the reverse.
- We believe that the kid who is interested in the insurance business should have the right to sample work on the twentieth floor of the Prudential Life Insurance building, as surely as the girl who wants to sell cosmetics or jewelry should be able to spend time on the first floor of Macy's.
- We believe that the boy who has an apparent aptitude and interest for architecture needs to experience work in a firm of architects or in a construction company, as surely as the youth who shows talent and a desire for landscaping needs to find out what it's like to work at a first-rate nursery and landscaping contractor.
- We believe that the girl who seems to have what it takes to become a great doctor should have a chance to see the field of medicine from the inside while she's still a teen-ager, as surely as the boy who seems to have what it takes to be a master plumber should have an opportunity to see plumbing from the vantage point of an apprentice.

Because the Career Education Center would offer on-the-job training and on-the-job observation in almost every conceivable occupation to which young people might aspire, the stigma that first attached itself to vocational education almost a century ago finally would be lifted.

- No longer would it be necessary for any student to choose between an academic track deemed socially acceptable by everybody and a vocational track considered unacceptable by almost everybody.
- No longer would any student need to feel embarrassed because he was among a very few engaged in a work-study program. In our system, we envision almost all young people electing to work part time somewhere, according to a schedule that best fits their total program.

- No longer would parents feel compelled to advise their children that the job training offered by the school is socially inferior dead-end training. Because their children would be training for jobs they *wanted* eventually on a full-time basis, perhaps at age seventeen or eighteen, or perhaps not until they were in their twenties and had spent a year traveling and had gone on to obtain their master's or doctoral degree.

- No longer would people be able to say that job training is only for boys and girls who can't cut it in the subjects that really count. Because a girl who is sailing along in the most advanced mathematics would be working part time at a local computer center, and a boy who knows only enough math to compute bar tabs and meal checks would be working part time at a restaurant down the street, learning to become a franchise manager.

The Career Education Center would be an autonomous institution under the governance of our Education Assembly, but it might be housed under the same roof with, or contiguous to, the Community Guidance and Evaluation Center.

Dr. Venn complained in his book that today's counselors don't do a very good job in helping students consider and select occupational goals. And we would cite a case of a boy who thought he wanted to be a forest ranger when he was in the eighth grade and so informed his counselor. Now a junior in high school, the boy has changed his mind a couple of times, but "forest ranger" is still his career choice insofar as the high school records are concerned. No counselor has ever wondered whether he changed his mind.

We have already described how our Community Guidance and Evaluation Center would operate, but it is necessary to reiterate here that the counselors, ombudsmen, and other personnel of the Guidance and Evaluation Center would be just as concerned about a child's career planning and work experience as they would be about his progress in learning the basic skills in reading and arithmetic. It is in the Community Guidance and Evaluation Center where children and their parents would map out career goals.

The staff of the Guidance and Evaluation Center would know, for instance, what careers a fourteen-year-old is interested in and has aptitude for on the basis of cumulative data and interviews with the child and his parents.

Also, the fourteen-year-old would have an opportunity to take advantage of the Greater Community Talent Bank maintained by the Community Guidance and Evaluation Center. The Talent Bank, the catalog of community residents willing to counsel youths about the work they do, would help the youth get some early vibrations and information about different fields he is interested in.

The counseling would be expert, and when the Guidance and Evaluation Center sent a youth over to the Career Education Center, both the youth and the Career Center would start with a wide-awake awareness of what he is most interested in and best suited for.

The centers together would help a youth sort out whim and curiosity about career fields from conviction and determination. They would help him make career decisions based on work experiences designed to

1. test cold assumptions and notions under the fire of reality;
2. provide concrete experiences among families of careers (health-medicine, communications, sales-merchandising, and so on);
3. promote a broader vision of the job opportunities within the career families;
4. provide a foundation upon which sensible decisions for career changes can be made.

The Career Education Center would *not* be a vocational school with an array of shops. For the most part, we would put the public school out of the job-training business. It might be necessary to provide instruction in typing and similar skills required as employment prerequisites. But the public school no longer would be responsible for building and equipping shops for instruction in machine tooling, printing, baking, auto repair, beauty culture, or dental assistance.

The school would not need to recreate at great expense a range of unreal job settings. Because boys and girls would learn machine tooling in a machine shop, would learn printing from a printer in his own shop, would work on cars in a service station, would learn the techniques on hair styling in a beauty salon, and would get training as a dental assistant at a college of dentistry, a dental clinic, or in a dentist's office.

No longer would a shop teacher have to wonder whether, after five, ten, or fifteen years, he was still in touch with his trade. No longer would his students have to fear that the techniques they are learning and the equipment they are using might be obsolete and irrelevant.

Students could not possibly be remote from the world of work because they would be immersed in it.

Our Career Education Center would not be in the masonry business, but would place students with master masons; it would not try to run an airline and teach pilots with lectures, but it would place students with airlines; it would not operate a bakery, but it would place students in bakeries. The center would build and staff no law school, but it would place students in law offices, courtrooms, and police precincts.

The Career Education Center would be under the direction of an elected board of parents and other community residents (including students). An executive officer would be in charge of operations. The center would have considerable fiscal freedom under the Education Assembly, and as such it would be an eligible agency to receive and expend federal and state funds earmarked for vocational education.

A major function of the center would be to draft agreements with industries, business establishments, government agencies, and professions in behalf of students aged fourteen to eighteen. These agreements would specify the responsibilities of the employer, the student employee, and the center. The center would negotiate with each employer the nature and frequency of supervision, the on-the-job training to be provided, salary, productivity expectations and measures, promotion possibilities and procedures, work standards, discipline, and dismissal procedures.

We would urge that students be employed as staff members of the center and participate fully in the negotiation and drafting of agreements for fellow students. The student employees also would serve as career supervisors, visiting students at their job. By employing students, the center would be practicing what it preached.

To see how the Career Education Center would function, how it would give vocational education dimensions it has never had before, we will follow the progress of two students.

● Meet Debra, age fourteen.

As a twelve-year-old, Debra had imagined herself modeling the expensive and latest fashions displayed on the runways pictured on her television screen. She dreamed of modeling swimsuits in the Bahamas in February, ski outfits in the Swiss Alps in July, and sport clothes in Las Vegas in April.

On one of her visits to the Community Guidance and Evaluation Center a year ago, Debra looked through the Talent Bank. She came up with the names of two models that live in the community and have volunteered to discuss career opportunities with interested youths. Upon Debra's request, a counselor at the center called both models to see whether an appointment could be made. One woman was out of the country; the other asked Debra to visit her at the agency where she was employed.

The meeting with the model was worked into Debra's schedule and the two of them spent a day together. The experience reinforced Debra's desire to be a model.

Shortly after her fourteenth birthday, Debra and her parents met with her counselor at the Guidance and Evaluation Center. During the interview, Debra displayed almost as much interest in the design of clothes as she did in modeling them. And the counselor sensitively but frankly discussed the uncertainty of Debra's future facial and body development, even though at fourteen she was tall, lean, and pretty.

The counselor suggested on the basis of the discussion that

Debra's work experience provide her with opportunities to talk with, observe, and assist dress designers and clothes buyers as well as models. Debra agreed.

At the Career Education Center, Debra met with a young career supervisor who had already received information about Debra from the counselor. After several meetings with the career supervisor and with two prospective employers, Debra decided on an agreement that placed her for a maximum ten hours a week for six months in a woman's clothes manufacturer in the city. The firm employs clothes designers and models, and store buyers come in periodically to see what the manufacturer is offering.

The personnel manager of the company agreed to let Debra work at two jobs. One required her to assist in dressing and fitting rooms used by models; the second required her to be on hand when buyers come in to run errands, serve coffee and buns, take messages, and so on.

The personnel manager also agreed to set up three or four special sessions during the six-month period where Debra could talk to and learn from designers, models, and buyers. Of course, these discussions were in addition to any contacts Debra made on her own while employed.

The agreement specified that the career supervisor would visit with Debra and her employer on the job every three weeks during the six-month period.

At the end of six months, Debra, the personnel manager, and the career supervisor were pleased with what had happened. Debra had done her assigned tasks well, but she had also done well on some unassigned tasks. For one thing, she became friendly with one of the dress designers who counseled her on the side—one night a week and sometimes on Saturday. Debra gave up the idea of modeling and is now concentrating on designing. The six-month agreement with the company has been extended another six months, but the new terms are that Debra will learn to operate a power sewing machine and will assist the head cutter. She reports to a designer.

In addition, Debra is spending two hours a week at our Community Arts Center, where fashion design is part of the program. Debra is learning there how to make her own clothes, and her mother has joined her.

● Meet Frank, age sixteen.

To lay in some necessary background, we should explain that the Career Education Center also places students in community service jobs, a local VISTA-like program encouraged by the Education Assembly. Like almost everything about our series of new public institutions for education, the public service is not required. But most students participate. Some volunteer a few hours a week in a city hospital, others are tutors for younger children in the schools, some work at a public family counseling center as clerks, others help pick up litter in city parks, and still others are volunteers in a variety of service jobs.

Most of the community service jobs tie in well with the students' paid work experience. For example, many of the kids who volunteer some time at the hospital also have, or contemplate, paid jobs there.

Frank came into the program late because he was so unsure of his future that he couldn't decide in what career field to work. Shortly after turning sixteen, Frank came to the Career Education Center and said he thought he might volunteer for something—anything that was open. A career supervisor asked if he would give a couple of hours a week over a three-month period to assist the United Fund drive in his city neighborhood. Without any particular enthusiasm, Frank accepted the job.

While serving on the United Fund drive, Frank met a copy editor from one of the city's daily newspapers. The editor also had volunteered his part-time services to the campaign. They had a number of long conversations, and the editor had Frank visit him a couple of times at the newspaper office.

Soon after the last visit to the newspaper office, Frank asked for a meeting at the Community Guidance and Evaluation Center with his mother and a counselor. The counselor was not very surprised at Frank's decision to test his ability and interest in news writing. In monitoring Frank's progress over the years, the counselor had observed that Frank wrote well and had a very inquisitive mind. He had once before suggested to Frank that he try his hand at writing for a newspaper, but the idea had to come from Frank. And Frank wasn't ready then.

At the Career Education Center, a career supervisor made an appointment with the copy editor and the newspaper's personnel manager. Frank and the supervisor discussed a nine-month agreement, fifteen hours a week.

The center is always careful to insure that the work experience for students is not unrelated to the work of the office or shop. For example, Frank's supervisor would not have condoned a job at the newspaper plant which required the boy simply to sweep up the wire room and empty waste baskets. That is not the way into this career and, despite Horatio Alger, it is probably not the way into any career. But floors need sweeping and baskets need emptying, and the young and inexperienced might do their share. The center's supervisors insist, however, that students are not solely employed as sweepers and emptiers, that such employment is very temporary and students move quickly on and up.

The agreement with the personnel manager of the newspaper specified that Frank would work under an assistant city editor, and that his tasks would vary. He would spend some time running copy from reporters to the copy desk; he would take edited copy and place it in cylinders to be shot through a pneumatic tube to the composing room; he would assist the library staff in clipping newspapers and filing articles; and he would occasionally go out on assignment with a city hall reporter, police reporter, or sports writer. And he probably would go get ten cups of coffee (four black, three with just milk, two with milk and sugar, and one heavy on the milk).

Frank would be expected to write at least two articles a week, either based on assignments with reporters or rewritten from wire copy that wasn't used in the paper. The articles would be critiqued either by the assistant city editor, who was his supervisor, or by the copy editor he had made as a friend.

The career supervisor came every two weeks to the newspaper

office, talked with the assistant city editor, the personnel manager, and Frank, and looked over the articles Frank had written along with their critiques.

Within two months, it was obvious to everyone that Frank was not happy and lacked either aptitude for, or interest in, newspaper reporting—or both. The assistant city editor suggested that Frank try writing copy with an advertising agency, or publicity and news releases for a public relations office.

Frank agreed to try the suggestion, and the career supervisor made a three-month agreement with the public relations office of a big utility. Before the career supervisor had made his first on-site visit, Frank stopped in to say he was really enjoying the work and liked the people in the office.

Today, many youths still move into a life career by accident, because Dad made a success of it, or because it was the first classified ad where the person on the phone said the job was still open.

We hope to change that insofar as possible through the Career Education Center.

- A boy could find out whether he was really inclined toward medicine before he got halfway through premed in college.
- A girl could find out through volunteer service that the career she had anticipated as a social worker will not do because her temperament simply is unsuited to the requirements of the job.
- A boy could prevent a lot of heartache by finding out that he was all thumbs in the construction trade skills that his uncle and cousins excelled in, but that he was valuable to their business because he enjoyed doing such things as bookkeeping and cost control—and did them very well.

In the beginning of this book, we described how America's schools have tinkered with reform and innovation, trying to make the school as an institution work well. Once again, we have tried to describe what happens when the institution becomes a hodgepodge of appended functions and the tinkering won't help.

The subtle, but mighty, forces at work in the institution impel behavior among the participants that is altogether contrary to their good intentions and the institution's official and avowed purposes.

We have proposed doing away with another of those dysfunctioning appendages—vocational education—and providing in its stead a new institutional delivery system for making career education an effective and vital experience in the life of every child.

The critics of vocational education have made these accusations:

1. Programs offered are too limited in scope, being largely in the skilled trades.
2. Programs include too few of America's youths.
3. Instruction tends to be isolated and technically obsolete.
4. Vocational education, being approved by everybody for someone else's children, is stigmatized as a program for the intellectually dull and the socially inferior. Because vocational education is a victim of class snobbery, the institution segregates "vokes" in the comprehensive school or sends them to a special school, thus refueling the age-old snobbery.
5. Teaching methods are poor and unrealistic.
6. The federal government, that once stultified change because of the conditions stipulated in its appropriations bills, now tries with less than success to reverse the advanced arteriosclerosis that afflicts vocational education.

Our Career Education Center would take the incredibly vast range of productive human labor in the community and make it the focus and also the locus of career education. We would provide a system that invites and encourages participation by every student, thereby erasing the existing snobbery.

By putting emphasis on training at the place of employment, we would insure against obsolescence. Finally, by once again involving students and their parents, we would create a firm foundation to undergird the system.

We believe the appendage called vocational education had to fail. It could not have happened any other way.

We believe the Career Education Center has to succeed. We don't think it can happen any other way.

Seven

Creating New Learning Forms

ON THE CAMPUS of Shippensburg State College in Pennsylvania, alumni and friends of the college have reconstructed the old Potato Point School, a one-room building that stood and served in the countryside outside the town of Newburg until 1954.

The school that once was filled with the sounds of children's learning echoes now to the sounds of tourists giving the curiosity a once-over. Children break loose from their parents to sit in the double desks and open and close and open and close the door to the pot-bellied stove.

Occasionally, a parent or grandparent will pause to remember how it was.

> There used to be boys and girls of all ages in this room; I guess maybe from six to fifteen or thereabouts. The teacher would go from one group or individual to another. And when he was busy, we'd work with each other. I remember tutoring a little girl in arithmetic nearly every day. I think I taught her more than the teacher.

The child will quickly grow tired of when-I-was-a-boy stories and beg to move along to the next attraction of the day. But first he may exclaim in disbelief: "Wow! You mean there were kids as young as me and as old as Davey and Jean in the same room? And *they* could have taught *me?* You must be kidding."

The Potato Point School opened its doors to the first mixed bag of children in the last year of the Civil War. For nearly a century, younger and older children learned side by side—learned what they had to learn and when it was time for them to learn it. As we have said over and over again, the institution compels the behavior of those in it, and the one-room school for children of many ages compelled the teacher to serve individual children according to their needs. It was a time when everybody knew what mankind always had known: *Each child differs from every other child, and some children are more intelligent than others. Furthermore, every child is brighter in some things than he is in others.*

And when the teacher was busy with one child, or two, or a group, the other children would work alone or together. They would share information and exchange ideas (and sometimes jokes and gossip). And the children who already had mastered multiplication taught it to those who hadn't; a boy who knew how to spell big words drilled a girl who didn't, and a fifteen-year-old girl read stories to a seven-year-old boy. Children helped each other because it was the natural thing to do; it was expected behavior in the one-room institution.

But at about the same time the mortar was setting between the bricks on the Potato Point School, schools that packaged children into grades and packaged learning the same way were beginning to go up like the factories of the Industrial Age in urban America. And in those schools, the teacher was expected by the institution to stand before children of the same age and teach the same thing to all. The new institution's ground rules said students didn't speak unless spoken to by the teacher; they did not speak at all to each other.

Today, the one-room school is very scarce, and what went on inside it either doesn't go on at all in the graded school of the 1970s or is labeled an innovation—a breakthrough.

For example, a 1970 announcement about a new project called the Cross-Age Helping Program (Center for Research on Utilization of Scientific Knowledge, University of Michigan) advised educators:

> The Cross-Age Helping Program is an exciting approach to the learning environment. Through it, older children are trained to help younger ones learn. The seven years of research and use which have gone into the preparation of these curriculum materials show

that properly trained older students can respond creatively and constructively to younger ones. Numerous benefits accrue to both the older and the younger students, including improved academic performance and better attitudes toward teachers, school, self, and others.

Seven years of research and use, indeed! More like 150 years of practice. And it worked year after year after year.

The alumni and friends of Shippensburg State College have restored the ancient Potato Point School as a tourist attraction to be examined and poked and occasionally appreciated. We also believe the good things of the past should be preserved for our progeny, but we do not propose restoration of brick walls, belfries, and black slate boards.

Instead, we strongly advocate—and it is central to all our proposals—the restoration everywhere of the age-old truths about children and about learning that were known and practiced intrinsically in the Potato Point School; in the little school outside Tuscaloosa, Alabama, in the thirties; and in some places still today.

What we want to reconstruct for tomorrow's children is what is left today to only a few. It remains in such places as the Monarch School in Montana. There, freelance writer Winthrop Griffith, looking at education in a one-room school for the first time, marveled at the behavior impelled by the institution. The teacher explained it to him, and he quoted her in his article in *The New York Times Magazine.*[1]

The children here have had a basically ungraded, flexible, independent study situation for years. There's no choice here, with kids at ten different so-called levels of learning. Those seventeen children [aged six to fourteen] are in one small room for almost seven hours each day. We are all involved with one another and we all learn from one another. We have to. I have only so much time and there's only so much space for all those children. I give each one of them as much individual attention as I can, but in one sense we are together all the time.

1. Winthrop Griffith, "A Daring Educational Experiment—The One–Room Schoolhouse," *The New York Times Magazine,* May 30, 1971.

When, at the bidding of Horace Mann and Henry Barnard and others, American education shifted to the graded school, teachers and students could no longer behave as they do in the Monarch School. The new institution dictated new behaviors.

Children tutoring each other in the one-room school became cheating and "disruptive behavior" in the graded school. Teaching individual children was forced by the one-room school setting, but it became nearly impossible to teach individuals in the graded school. Even the furniture in the graded school contributed to the new behavior. In the one-room school two or three children would share the same bench, but in the graded school each child sat alone.

We would restore the old behaviors still maintained in Monarch —restore them to education in New York City; Winnetka, Illinois; Atlanta; Cherry Creek, Colorado; and Los Angeles.

And everywhere else in the United States of America.

But not just in the one place called school.

Already we have stripped the graded school, taking away appendages that have not worked well for children and giving them over to new institutions that would make them work well for children —and in most cases for all residents of the community. And the self-evident truths about people and learning would once again flourish there.

But the school—that three-story brick building in your neighborhood, or that sprawling pile of veneered cement blocks that children reach mostly by bus and car—is not only what's left after peeling off the appendages.

At least our Education Assembly would see more than one basic learning institution called a school. Its concern would be the education needs of all ages and not just the operation of schools. The Education Assembly would discover, develop, and sponsor many new institutions and programs designed to bring all learning to the people.

Given the challenge of providing learning experiences for children aged one to five, the typical board of education today would focus its attention on how to do it in the existing school setting. Its questions probably would not range much beyond these: "How many teachers will be needed?" "How many additional school classrooms will be needed, and can these be found or must they be constructed?" "What's the projected enrollment?" and "What will be the cost?"

The Education Assembly, on the other hand, would want to know such things as the precise need, the difficulties involved in satisfying the need, the alternative means for satisfying the need, what ideas parents have about learning programs for their infants, and the potential impact of such programs on family life. And the assembly surely would want to know if one of the best ways to provide learning for infants is to bring education into a home setting where family members might be involved in the learning process.

In the next chapter, we will describe alternatives to the school, even as the school itself will provide alternative learning methods within its walls.

We would not blindly reconstruct the one-room school. This institution had its virtues, which we have described, but it also had serious limitations as the sole instructional instrument of its day.

But even one hundred years ago, when one-room schools began to close down and children and teachers shifted to larger schools, what was good about the old schools could have been transferred into the new institutions.

Instead of children being sorted out by age and placed into grades numbered one through twelve, the children could have remained mixed in age. Instead of classrooms for six-year-olds in grade one and classrooms for eleven-year-olds in grade six, there could have been classrooms for children aged six to eleven.

Now, a century later, we propose doing just that in the minischool that is one of our institutions for basic education.

We would have minischools for children aged three or four up to age eleven. And most of the time children aged six to eleven would be mixed in the same rooms, doing different things, but learning from each other and helping each other.

We would have minischools for children aged twelve to eighteen. And most of the time they would be mixed, doing different things, but learning from one another and helping each other.

These institutions are called minischools for two reasons. First, we have taken away most of the functions that have accumulated over the years to make them maxi. Second, we would reduce the size of most schools from what they normally are today. The minischool for younger children, for example, would include as few as 150 children but not much more than 300 children.

The minischool for older children might accommodate up to 600, but not many more.

We fully recognize that there are some schools with enrollments in excess of 1,000 where children succeed by today's standards. But students in such schools do well mostly because there are teachers who have learned to overcome the institution and the behaviors it compels.

The institution only nudges people into submission to its rules, it doesn't beat them into submission with whips and chains. So teachers can offer learning for individuals; they can show affection toward individuals; they can demonstrate great understanding of individuals. But it is extremely difficult and wearing to persist against the institution; it is easier to do what the institution subtly compels and to accept its rewards for submission.

There are teachers all over the country who have the exceptional talent and the exceptionally strong determination to break the restraints that keep most of their colleagues from setting children free to learn. But we have said right along that the institution should not be designed so that only superpeople can thrive in it. The institution should be designed so that it generates the kind of behavior by each person that encourages learning by each person.

Our minischools would be operated by a board of parents, teachers, and students under the overall direction of the Education Assembly and its administrative arm. The minischool board would hire staff and whatever clerks and custodians were needed to keep records and maintain facilities. Employment standards and Civil Service regulations established by the Education Assembly and the state would control these hiring practices.

Today's principal might not find a familiar role in our minischools. The elimination of all the appendages and specialists would make it unnecessary for him to be a ringmaster. The educational program would be as varied as the children and teachers engaged in learning, thereby diminishing the principal's role as manager and enforcer of standardized curriculum. Whether he would be executive officer for the minischool board, chairman of a teaching unit, a teacher, or a supervising learning specialist would be decided by experience and by the principal's own talents.

For as long as anyone can remember, children have commenced kindergarten only at the beginning of the school year in which they became age five. But the standard is complicated by the additional requirement that the kindergartner must reach the age of five prior to October 1, or December 15, or some other arbitrary date. Presumably, children born on October 2 or December 16 are unready for whatever it is the school has to offer—ipso facto.

But we would propose that children enter the minischool on their birthday, or the next day. We recognize, of course, that all parents will not want their children entering a minischool at age three, four, or five, and they should not be required to do otherwise. But suppose parents do want their three-year-old enrolled in a program geared to his needs. The child might begin on September 5, November 2, May 1, or July 28.

Starting in July would be no problem because none of our institutions would take a vacation. They would be open year-round.

The time a child would spend in a minischool in relation to the time scheduled at other institutions and in other programs would be in accord with his learning plan. The learning plan would result from an agreement between the child, his parents, and counselor.

But no child probably would spend more than three hours on any day at a minischool.

Most children don't spend much more than three hours in basic education today when one considers time spent in special subject areas, electives, club activities, study halls, recess, and cafeteria.

But most children would not be in the minischool for three hours in a row every day. On some days, a child might not be in the minischool at all, his learning plan calling for a full day once a week at the Community Arts Center. On another day, the child might be in the minischool from 9 to 10:30 A.M. and again from 2 to 3 P.M. The intervening time might be spent at the other institutions, at work, or engaged in a scheduled experience in some other place: up to his knees in a river testing for pollution, taking private ballet lessons, interviewing the police chief, and so on.

For those who need routine and regularity—and this would include many of the younger children—such diversity could be confusing. A more stable pattern, therefore, would be established for them.

Before talking in chapter 8 about the alternatives to learning within the minischool and the alternatives to the minischool itself, it is important to talk about the climate of the minischool and about the learning materials it would make available, and how they might be used.

Through the years, the school has been concerned with the effect of the instruction in the three Rs on students, and it has found ways —albeit many of them are inaccurate and inexpert—to measure the impact of the teaching.

But the institution has not been very much aware of how the behavior it has compelled has affected the children. Awareness only started when the institution showed concern over the reasons for students dropping out, and when today's outspoken youth began talking back to their elders and telling them just how the climate of the school was suffocating them, driving them to drugs, turning them off, or just boring them.

The truth is that the school always has had a tremendous impact on the lives of those who have spent most of their developing years in it.

For those persons who are concerned that today's school should not attempt to teach character traits and should confine itself to the academic three Rs, the answer is that no institution housing childern five or more hours a day can fail to affect deeply the child's psyche for better or worse, consciously or unconsciously, planned or unplanned. The school teaches character traits subliminally, atmospherically, and indirectly, as well as directly according to the lesson plan. But however the teaching is done, it penetrates deeply and permanently, and children soon learn how to feel about themselves.

- Children learn quickly whether the institution and its members consider them to be stupid or smart, whether they are liked or unliked, and whether there is a good chance to succeed or whether they face certain failure. The formation of the self-concepts begins with the earliest exposure in the first grade to the climate and behaviors created and nurtured by the graded school that sees masses of children to be managed.
- Children learn to compete against each other for good marks. They compare their mark with others, because they know their work has been compared to others in the class.
- They compete for such rewards as bright stars, tokens, and special privileges. ("The good boys and girls may go to the library." "The people who are quiet and in their seats will be excused for recess before everybody else.")
- They compete for teachers' praise and affection.
- Teachers ask questions of the whole class, or of individual children in front of the whole class. Out of a typical class of twenty-five, perhaps five always will answer or frantically wave their arms to be recognized, and they usually will have the answer the teacher wants. But ten children—nearly half the class—will try to avoid answering or being called on. They have discovered that they seldom, if ever, have the answer the teacher wants, and so exposure of themselves before their peers is an embarrassment they prefer not to risk.

In the one-room school, individual students found it difficult to compete against the class; it was an unintended consequence of an institution that mixed children of different ages, capabilities, and abilities. Not only didn't the institution call upon them to compete, its social structure made it necessary and desirable that they tutor each other.

In the graded school, individual students compete against each other and the class because the institution makes it happen that way. Because the children are nearly all of the same age, the institution has presumed that they all have mostly the same capabilities. And so the teacher is required to deal with them as a class and not as individuals. They are taught en masse, tested en masse, and questioned en masse.

One must compete simply to be recognized as an individual.

The competition is so keen that students generally are forbidden or afraid to help each other. Those who violate the rule may be silenced or punished by the institution, or they may feel they cheated themselves because the one they helped has pulled ahead in the race for marks, class rank, points, pats on the head, smiles, and privileges.

If America's teachers were polled and asked if they ever taught children to feel stupid, all but a sensitive few would emphatically and honestly answer no. And yet across the country there are children who learn in school that they are stupid or dull. Often they are never able to overcome the self-image.

The child will judge himself harshly because his performance doesn't stand up well against his classmates, and because he is not eligible for advanced classes, the honor roll, and the ranks of those considered "good college material." Perhaps worse, he may castigate himself for having been eliminated from the unwritten list of students upon whom teachers shower attention, and the unpublished social register—or pecking order—known to every student.

Competition in our society is a seemingly universal aspect of human behavior. Those who argue, as we do, against the schools' use of techniques designed to compel children to attempt to excel over one another do so because they and we are aware of a number of dangers and negative consequences that can result.

As we have indicated, competition as a tool to induce learning is of limited appeal and effect. It simply does not work for most children. Leaders in politics, business, and sports, by virtue of their own status, find pedagogical attacks on competition among children to be subversive of the very foundation of our society. They have arrived by successful exploitation of their talents, coupled with a driving ambition—an acutely developed capacity to compete. ("By God! I overcame everything and everybody to get where I am today.")

But competition is a motivator, a rewarder, an energizer for only the talented few. It leaves the majority—frequently the vast majority —unmotivated, deflated, and unrewarded. It teaches them noninvolvement: "If at first you don't succeed, don't try again."

Our view of the role of competition in the design and organization of learning institutions, therefore, is that it should not be prohibited; in our society that is impossible. Instead, it should be exploited as a technique for motivating group behavior—team versus team, rather than individual versus individual.

The schools use competition to excess usually because they have failed to develop and utilize a better technique. They have not constructed patterns and activities for learners that use other techniques known to be powerful stimulants to human energy.

For example, groups of children learn readily to cheer each other on. Groups of children learn to praise their companions' achievement. Individuals who chart and measure their own growth in body, skills, dexterities, traits, habits, and social competencies become self-energizing. They compete against themselves, doing better today than yesterday and better tomorrow than today.

These truths about human behavior have been neglected. The graded school reduced them to abstract verbalizations. Human generosity and children's quick affections were squeezed out as inappropriate behaviors for a competitive classroom, and rhetoric and preachment were substituted for genuine practice.

In our minischool, competition between children and between individuals and a class would be diminished—and for pretty much the same reasons it was not easy in the one-room school. Children of different ages and capabilities would be mixed in the same rooms, impelling teachers to look at them as individuals and making it natural and easy for children to help each other.

The motto for each child might well be: I am my brother's tutor.

Children would not be tested and rewarded according to how well they perform in class rank and competition. The makers of educational materials would no longer decide what results should be expected from their packages for fifth graders or tenth graders. Children in the minischool would be evaluated—and would evaluate themselves—on the basis of how well they learn what they set out to learn. There would be no penalty, no stigma, no guilt associated with trying again if at first one did not succeed. Seven-year-olds are now largely confined to a second-grade classroom with second-grade books. We would uncork them to read at skill levels far beyond that normally associated with their age.

In our minischool, teachers and other adults would be counseled and encouraged to behave honestly with children.

In today's school there is much behavior that is artificial, and the masquerade invites dishonest behavior and distrust from children. Many of these artificial behaviors derive from the best of intentions. The schools mistake the guides of good mental health to mean that teachers must never chastise, never be negative, never speak frankly, never speak angrily. The result is bottled up antagonisms, costumed friendliness, false praise, and concealed negativism. This is unhealthy for the adult and for the children at whom it is directed. But it is only the good people, the well-intentioned people who are guilty of being artificial in their behavior.

Teachers sometimes pretend excitement when everyone knows there is nothing to be excited about, and pleasure when there is nothing to be pleased about. They shower praise or administer pats on the head when everyone knows no such attention has been earned. They are blasé when some display of emotion is plainly called for.

Very young children sense the truth of adults' feelings and react to them instead of to their masquerades. A teacher stops at his classroom door before entering to caution himself not to allow the heat of a recent argument with fellow teachers to affect his behavior with his students. But the caution serves only to produce a superficial good cheer. After about thirty minutes, a little girl pulls on his pants leg and inquires, "Why are you angry at us today?"

Because children's early instinctive capacity to sense emotional truth is followed by a growing ability to detect ever more subtle forms of adult put-ons, the schools increasingly are criticized by young people as being hypocritical institutions. There are thousands upon thousands of students in our high schools who openly express distrust of some or many of their teachers.

Those engaged in introducing sensitivity training—behavior training—into the schools say over and over again that their main task is to replace distrust among participants with trust.

Teachers and other adults in our minischool (and in the other institutions, of course) would be expected to display emotions honestly, without unnecessarily hurting or embarrassing a child. Children can, and must, be told "no" and "stop." But chastisement in front of an audience is humiliation; so, correction should be attempted in private. Only emergencies threatening physical harm warrant public censure of children.

- When the occasion calls for joy, minischool teachers would be free to express it as exuberantly as the children—up to and including hand-clapping and other outward displays of pleasure.
- When the occasion calls for anger, they would be free to shout it out of their system as children do. They will know that suppressed anger leaks out as sarcasm, and usually it is far more damaging.
- When the occasion calls for praise, teachers would freely give it. But they will not tell everybody that everything they do is "great," "very, very nice," "the best of all."
- When the occasion calls for sadness or disappointment, they would not ignore and trespass on the children's mood by pretending to be cheerful. They would not find a silver lining when the children realize that only a black cloud exists (even though they are inwardly aware that it will eventually pass over). To comfort a child's despair is honest; to suppress his tears his damaging.

Children respond honestly to honest emotions; they trust those who demonstrate that their emotions can be trusted. We would create a climate that encourages honesty and trust, and would seek an end to that behavior—usually unintentional—by which many American schools discourage both virtues.

Today's youths are probably praised more, criticized more, examined more, and misunderstood more than any generation of young people in this century. But in any case we seem to have a generation which finds it easier than most generations to express emotions freely. They abhor what they see as artificiality and hypocrisy in life. They also abhor war and those who make it and find glory and reward in it.

Many have rejected the material goals of their elders in favor of a simple life. Many have rejected the pious worship of God on Sunday morning in order to revive a communal and primitive Christianity.

It was largely at the insistence of today's young people that the nation took a second and serious look at what is happening to our environment. They are saying that what is good for General Motors may be deadly for people. Because of the simple virtues they seek, they have turned to handicrafts as one road to the good life. They have rightly concluded that the arts are not for snobs and spectators, but for doing and using by everybody.

But today's young people also are products of Early Spock—the 1950s doctrine that admonished parents not to scold their offspring except in the most severe cases of hostile behavior, because discipline was potentially damaging to the child.

Early Spock has contributed to the Now Generation, young people who want gratification of their appetites—now, who want answers to all questions—now, who want solutions to all problems—now. For them, later is never.

Many among the generation in today's high schools rebel against the authority of institutions, against society's authority figures, and even blindly against the older generation. Bettelheim attributes this to the absence of adequate authority figures in the home.

A natural condition of adolescence is to seek emancipation from paternal domination—what used to be called in more innocent days the cutting of the apron strings—the adolescent revolt.

But the father's role in many families has been castrated. There was a time when a child could count on seeing his father every day; now he may see his father only on weekends, and not always then. There was a time when the child could easily understand what his father did for a living; now it is equally hard for the child to comprehend his father's role on an assembly line or his role in the executive suite of a conglomerate. Father may no longer be the symbol of strength, no longer the court of last resort, no longer the model for maleness, no longer present.

And so the child grown into a youth and finding it necessary to break away from the authority of his father is confused, frustrated. There is little or no authority in the home to be emancipated from. Consequently, he seeks emancipation from the high school principal, the police, the teacher, people over thirty, and institutions created by adults. And sometimes this public rebellion is violent.

In bygone days there were pubertal rites that ended boyhood and girlhood and ushered in manhood and womanhood. And the transformation was real. Those who passed puberty were expected to bear the responsibilities and assume the roles of adults.

Today the arrival of puberty is almost meaningless in society. Religious denominations may conduct confirmation or bar mitzvah ceremonies, but even the promise of full acceptance into the life of the church or synagogue is not fulfilled. Witness the continuing efforts to organize youths into their own groups, to promote special youth services, to find ways "to involve" the youths.

Childhood is unnaturally prolonged by a society that customarily denies its young people entrance into the adult world until they reach their early twenties. Consequently, the youths form their own subculture frequently hostile to accepted adult culture.

It also has become increasingly difficult for youths to find adult employment in their postpuberty years—one more monumental exasperation for those who would try to accept and enter the adult world.

To a great extent, our Career Education Center would overcome a fundamental part of youths' frustration at being excluded from adulthood through its work experience programs for young people aged fourteen to eighteen. Work, job satisfaction, wages in some cases, and the sense of contribution in others are all necessary feelings and reactions in the healthy maturing of our young. We are not trying to glorify the old Calvinist work ethic, but we are persuaded

that between fourteen and eighteen productive activity—both volunteer and paid as a member of the adult world—is a fundamental
need in the transition from childhood dependence to adult independence and competence.

We would also deal with youthful behavior that says, "Gimme—
now," "Do it—now," "Make peace—now," "Destroy all that is cor-
rupt—now," and "Make love—now." The behavior that is simply
petulant one day can become hostile the next.

We would try to give young people a new perspective on life
through new social science units designed to show children and
youths how history has been a constant struggle by Man to be free.
We would show that history has produced few true villains and
true heroes, that little has happened that has been wholly good or
wholly evil, why it is that Man can weep over a dog struck down
by a car and only yawn at reports of racial genocide.

Such units would look at all civilizations in terms of an individual's
relationship to other people, to his gods, to his government, and to
the land. We would have our children study war as an instrument
of terror and degradation, and invite them to question its employment in the pursuit of noble causes through a careful examination
of the revolutions and revulsions of the ages.

One of the anticipated learnings from what we propose is that
history is a mix of events and people that produced both tyranny
and liberty—sometimes simultaneously. We want the great and
not-so-great of the ages to take on flesh and blood, rather than to
appear as one-dimensional stick figures that are either only right
or only wrong.

We hope to prevent the disillusionment that has come to so many
youths and adults when they discover that history has been dis-
torted in their classrooms, that their textbooks have exaggerated,
left many things unsaid, or simply falsified.

In the end, we hope our children would see that Man has sought
to be free, to love, and to find and enjoy beauty, but that the search
has gone in many directions and taken many forms.

We have lived with the myth of the melting pot in America. We
have assumed with a snob-like arrogance that "they" needed to be
assimilated. Moynihan and Glaser have now documented their

judgments that many immigrants have not been melted into the larger society.

As persons concerned with the healthy development of children and with the health of our society, we are pleased that the assimilation of the tired, poor huddled masses has not been altogether successful and complete. Because the process of melting down—with the schools acting as the crucible—taught our children to be ashamed of their parents, their manners, their customs and costumes, their beliefs, their accents, even their less frequent use of soap.

In the liberal tradition of the country, generosity and goodwill are stimulated. But from the depths of ancient feelings toward those who are different come fear, suspicion, and the willingness to suppress.

We are determined that the overarching and oldest goal of America—the creation of a nation of free peoples—shall govern the content and learning of the social sciences in our new educational institutions.

We are persuaded that diversity can only be honored as the whole is recognized by its parts, and the parts are free to honor themselves in harmony with the whole.

Unfortunately, societies, cultures, and nations seldom have allowed diversity. People of minor races, religions, and cultures have existed in history as victims, objects of social scorn, scapegoats for a country's ills, or its slaves.

Our revolutionary doctrine that a people governed shall be the government, was somewhat flawed at the start. As Abigail Adams reminded her "friend" John when he boasted of the new Constitution as a new advance for Man in his search for freedom, that much-revered document omitted half of the populace of the thirteen states—all women, all black slaves, and most men who did not own property.

Now, 200 years later, we are undertaking to grant—but slowly—full and equal status to females, blacks, and the poor. It has taken us this long to hear the lament of Abigail Adams over the loud din caused by a nation growing great and prosperous.

In the latest phase of the uneven quest for recognition and freedom, ethnic groups have hyphenated themselves to the bold word "power" and are calling loudly for racially autonomous institutions. The liberal movement to end segregation based upon law and racial hostility is even being attacked as a new form of racial erasure. Integration is seen as a new form of submission to the majority. So, there are strong efforts to produce schools of black studies, oriental studies, Mexican studies, and Indian studies—and female studies.

Insofar as these movements represent educational efforts to give minority children a sense of identity, a sense of pride in their parents and in their ethnic differences from the dominant culture, we would be helpful and supportive. Insofar as the separatist movements become—as historically they always have—hostile and teachers of hate toward the majority culture and its adherents, then we must attempt change.

This will not be easy. To maintain one's heritage in a minority group has seldom been possible without regarding the rest of the world with a defensive antagonism.

Our new social science units, therefore, would enable all children to learn that Man's need and quest for freedom transcend the special and parochial loyalties of race, minority defensiveness, and majority abusiveness. But all the while we would protect and encourage pride in ethnic differences.

Although all men share a like destiny, our sense of interdependence has been weak. But in our common freedom—equally enjoyed —we shall find the cohesion our society needs. In our continued diversity without discrimination, we shall reach a new maturity— an ability to respect and treasure our differences.

These are the lessons we would offer our troubled, confused, and doubting young people. They should be the greatest of all lessons to be learned.

We would expect that a visitor to either the minischool for young children or the minischool for older children will find behaviors that are honest, that are accepting of others, and that are evidence of the participants' understanding of Man's varied behavior.

We also would expect the visitor to find new kinds of educational materials—designed and stored for learning and learners.

In today's school, the materials of education and their use often are not compatible with how children behave and learn. And not infrequently they are stored in such ways as to discourage even the limited uses for which they were intended.

As a visitor, walk into what would be considered a good, modern kindergarten.

Below the windows which form one wall of the classroom are shelves and cabinets standing about thirty inches off the floor under the sill of the windows. There is a green chalkboard across the front of the room, with the teacher's desk and chair centered in front of it or slightly off to the side. A piano is against one wall. Also against a wall is a counter with a sink and attached drinking fountain. There are some cabinets below the countertop at the children's level, and some cabinets above the counter accessible to the teacher. There is a large storage closet for supplies. To one side of the carpeted room are five or six round tables with a corresponding number of small chairs at each of them.

The children are at play in this room. Building blocks are being used, large wooden trucks are being pushed and occasionally ridden, dolls are being placed in and taken out of carriages, painting with watercolors and fingerpaint is going on. The shelves under the windows are bursting with assorted toys, games, and boxes of things—including broken pieces of crayons that were new and whole at the start of the year.

In one place there are girls playing with miniature pots and pans at a miniature stove. Nearby, against the wall, are stacked long rectangular boxes designed to resemble bricks.

As the teacher looks anxiously, a boy heads for the stack of play bricks. Because of their location against the wall next to the miniature stove, the boy is required to disturb the girls' play in his effort to get to the bricks.

There are ten bricks, and the boy begins stacking them. He sets up three in a row, then begins to build on top of each one. By the time he has three stacks of three bricks, the piles are wobbling. The boy sees that the addition of the tenth brick on either of the stacks will send the bricks crashing to the floor. Like most boys, he is not at all opposed to seeing a stack of anything tumble magnificently to the floor. But he is not ready for that yet. He wants to build a wall first.

He takes down all the bricks and begins again by laying out three bricks. But this time he sees what someone in ancient times saw with probably the same degree of surprise and delight. The next row of bricks won't wobble if they overlap the first row. He jumps with the joy of a creator.

But there is again cause for frustration. The sixth brick will form a pyramid and there will be no room for the other four bricks. He examines the situation. Then, as though he had just discovered how to bridge the River Kwai, he places the sixth and seventh bricks on either side of the fourth and fifth bricks. They hang over a little precariously, but he has discovered how to solve his problem —how to build a wall. He makes happy sounds; he bubbles and chortles. They are the most beautiful sounds children can utter.

The visitor sits down at a table and pulls from the shelves under the sill a box containing upper and lower case letters of the alphabet and the numbers. The pieces are made of plywood and each measures about two inches. A little girl comes over. "I can make my name," she says. "It's Debbie." The visitor asks whether she would like to make her name. "Sure," she says with a slight look of exasperation that implies the visitor should have known immediately that that was her intention.

Debbie dips her hand into the box. Although the letters are large, the grand mix of A to Z, a to z, and 1 to 9 look like dried alphabet soup. It is not easy to find what one is looking for.

Debbie, who is spelling her name in capital letters, begins looking for a second B. There isn't one. After waiting to the edge of her interest, the visitor suggests a lower case b and she reluctantly agrees. Later she looks for a second capital E, and there isn't one. So, the visitor suggests a lower case e.

When her name is finished, Debbie looks at it with disgust. "I don't like my name that way; I don't like the way it looks. That's a stupid box."

Suddenly, the Cleanup Chord is sounded on the piano by the

teacher. It's time to return to the usual business of working or listening en masse. Children with broken pieces of crayons put them away in their containers; the girls playing with their miniature pots and pans put them in their proper place; the boy dismantles his brick wall and restacks the boxes against the wall next to the miniature stove, and the visitor replaces the "stupid" boxful of wooden letters and numbers in the Fibber McGee closet that is the storage area below the windows.

You have been in one of our best, modern kindergartens, but there is much that goes on inside it that is not sound educationally.

- To begin with, the materials have been stored to satisfy adult concepts of good housekeeping, not to invite children's use. (And this kind of out-of-the-way, inappropriate storage of educational materials extends through all of the grades of today's schools.)
- There are no good lessons to be learned by frustrated children searching through a box of broken crayons for the right one.
- There are no good lessons to be learned by a frustrated child trying to find letters of the alphabet and numbers in a "stupid" box that mixes them all together and doesn't even supply two of a kind.
- There are no good lessons to be learned by requiring a boy to return the bricks to the stack against the wall.
- How much better if the materials had been stored so as to invite learning instead of to frustrate it.
- We would purchase fat crayons and then place them standing up in holes drilled in a simple wooden disc.
- We would construct a box in which each of the letters and digits fit in an appropriate place.
- We would allow . . . no, we would agree with the intuitive wisdom of the boy showing us where the bricks belong for the next learning to occur.

All storage must be seen through the eyes of the learner. And so must the materials themselves. It is absurd, for instance, not to supply half bricks as well as whole ones. How else is a boy to discover brick laying as some genius in history did millennia ago. It is inappropriate to make children play with miniature pots and pans when they have long been playing with their mother's pots and pans. The unnecessary miniaturization creates an artificial preciousness.

We would design materials for children's use and locate them where children will see them, want them, and can get at them to use in their own ways. And these materials would be so varied as to cater to all the senses.

Children don't just learn by seeing or listening. They learn also by putting their hands into sand and paint, by touching animals and people. There is learning when pollution and perfume are smelled, when carrots and paste are tasted.

Each child learns through his own particular combination of senses, and so educational materials must be able to satisfy the different senses.

In the past, the schools have tended to rely excessively on the teacher's voice alone, on the book alone, the movie alone, the overhead projector alone, or the record alone. But mostly the teacher talked alone. We are suggesting that most learning materials be so conceived as to combine in one package things that can be read, and listened to, and felt—and maybe smelled or tasted.

And the materials have to be designed so that individual children may use them as they suit their learning styles. This is different from merely saying the materials must allow children to proceed at their own speed.

The programmed materials packaged in little steps that are supposed to allow children to go along as their ability warrants sometimes are not all that far from the lock-step approach of the most didactic teacher. We say the learner cannot be so confined. He must be free to move forward and backward through materials in his own idiosyncratic fashion. He must be free to learn the steps at random, not in the sequential order the overly programmed material dictates.

We would provide materials where sequential progress is possible, but on the learner's terms. The materials can be approached in different ways; learning goals will vary for individual learners, and the learner will be able to test himself as he progresses.

The television program "Mission Impossible" begins each segment with the main character coming upon a small tape recorder hidden in a phone booth, men's room, or glove compartment of a car. He switches it on: "Good morning, Mr. Phelps," the tape begins. It goes on to describe some horrendous plot being hatched in a foreign capital or stronghold of organized crime. Accompanying the tape is a package containing pictures of the good guys and bad guys involved in the plot and necessary charts, maps, and diagrams to enable a daring rescue or narrow escape.

Mr. Phelps is not ordered to mobilize his team for action. He's offered an out. The instructions on the tape are to proceed "should you accept the assignment." When was the last time you heard that in school?

We conceive of some packages of materials that might include a small tape describing what the components of the package are and what some of the learning possibilities and goals are (recognizing that there are many others that learners will see and set for themselves with the same materials).

The learner proceeds with some or all of the package only if he accepts the assignment. And he accepts it on his terms.

● Meet a learner. Call him Henry.

Pollution of the environment is the umbrella under which Henry is studying basic chemistry and biology.

He goes to one of the rooms in a minischool where there is displayed and ready for immediate use a rich assortment of equipment for scientific probing, experimenting, examining, testing, and discovering.

There also is a card catalog listing a wide variety of learning packages available in that room, in other rooms, in other minischools, and in the community library.

Henry finds a listing for a learning package that appeals to him, that seems to suit his needs at this particular time in his studies. As briefly described, the materials seem to offer him the necessary information and experiences to take him the next several steps in his learning.

Henry goes to a bank of shelves upon which are a number of containers approximately nine inches wide, twelve inches long, and three inches deep. They are all marked as indicated by the catalog. Henry selects the one he has picked from the catalog.

Inside the container is a large envelope, a cassette, a film strip, and several microscope slides.

Henry inserts the cassette in a machine available in the room:

> This package of materials deals with pollution of the water by phosphates. The envelope contains the instructions you will need and describes the equipment and chemicals you may want to use in conducting your own tests. The film strip demonstrates how to use the equipment.
>
> You may want to conduct the experiments with other learners. If you do, there is a special set of instructions that will help group activities.
>
> The slides are for a standard microscope and show evidence of water pollution. You may wish to study them first, or simply use them to compare with water samples you collect. (Of course, Henry is free not to look at the slides at all.)
>
> Should you undertake all or some of the tasks described in the envelope, you may wish to test what you have learned. There are several self-tests in the envelope. You may select the ones suited to the assignments you handle and your learning goals. There are also self-tests for other individuals should you choose to work with a group.

Among the things Henry finds in the envelope, in addition to what already has been described, is a map showing several locations along area rivers and streams which are most appropriate for studying the effects of phosphates in water. There is a listing of scientists and health officials at local and regional levels whom the learner may wish to consult. There are also photocopies of some pertinent data taken from books, magazines, and scientific journals (plus references to other materials).

It is, of course, obvious that we have shifted the emphasis in education from instruction directed by teachers to learning directed by learners.

This concept needs a philosophy to undergird it, and this is ours.

1. The learner needs goals for his learning, and his goals must prevail.
2. The learner, to be motivated to learn, must recognize that the learning materials are important to him, necessary to his achieving his goals.
3. Learning is accomplished in many ways. Learning is derived from solving problems, writing, analyzing data, observing, interviewing, and listening. Learning sometimes involves taking a complex thing or idea apart into its many pieces. Reconstructing a whole thing or idea is learning. Helping a student take these small steps toward larger goals is very effective learning. We would hope to see the expanded use of close-circuit TV for the purpose of studying the characteristics and skills of the learning process, much as a football team uses a film to analyze blocking and tackling skills, learning each small step that, when put together, represents the whole skill called blocking or tackling.
4. The learner must be given the opportunity to learn in a realistic setting. To learn well, Henry needed to go to a river or stream to see water pollution firsthand. And the learner then must have the chance to practice his learning in a realistic setting. One of the last steps for Henry in the unit described might be to take his findings about water pollution to a governmental agency or to the news media as additional evidence of a worsening condition.
5. The learner needs to get feedback as he learns, so that he does not consistently repeat errors or proceed along paths that are dead ends. Teacher guidance, self-tests, and tutorial help from other learners are ways for him to obtain such feedback.
6. The learner must have rewards appropriate to his achieve-

ments. This might mean that work he has done is shared with his peers or with the community at large. It might mean simply comments from a person whose judgment and wisdom the learner respects. For example, if Henry eventually comes up with some interesting findings in his research, it might be ample reward if they are accepted with thanks by the head of the science department at a nearby college. And under our earliest of requirements, Henry's family would be involved. We would restore parental pride.

7. Learning is a step-by-step approach, but not a lock-step approach. The learner must learn by degrees, but the degrees are not the same for all learners, and the sequence of steps is not the same for all learners.

We would resurrect the simple truths and the one learning style that nearly died with the genocide of one-room schools. But we would bring them back into new settings designed with far more knowledge of how children learn, with far more sophisticated learning materials, and an extraordinary expansion of the curriculum.

The institution dictates how its participants will behave, and we learned from the one-room school that the institution that mixes ages and talents produces desirable behavior. With that insight, we have designed a whole new family of educational institutions and programs.

We intend that their form and structure will impel learners and adults associated with them to learn, and to learn those things and values we as a culture esteem.

But most important, we hope that we will have set in motion a process and an institution to replace the existing school board that can, and will, generate ever more effective institutions for learning.

Eight

More—Not of the Same

How do we envision children learning through this new design for education we have conceived?

Let us count the ways.

But before the counting begins, we want to emphasize that our listing of ways in which children—and adults—might learn is not meant to be exclusive. Far from it!

Already we have said that it is our intention that the Education Assembly would be concerned with providing education, not with operating schools.

Consequently, we envision the assembly authorizing a wide range of learning approaches. Such paths to learning would be limited only by the limitations of creative imagination and the standards of relevance and feasibility.

And we would insist that the assembly be as free to subtract from the list of alternatives to learning as it is free to add to the list.

American public education has suffered too long from the chronic paralysis that prevents people in authority from terminating those learning methods, those curricula, those practices that simply are not working effectively for learners.

We would expect that our Education Assembly would alter or eliminate those learning operations that are not satisfying the learners' needs and providing the services that were originally intended. And if those operations should include any of the alternatives we are about to suggest, so be it.

155

We introduced the minischool in the last chapter—one for children up to age eleven and one for youths aged twelve to eighteen. We described the kinds of behavior that would be generated and encouraged, and we talked about some of the new learning materials that might be developed and used to good advantage.

The minischool for younger children would contain children of different ages just as the one-room school did, but it would mix them in ways never dreamed of in the days when the little red schoolhouse flourished in America.

One of those ways would be the new approach in the British infant schools, the so-called open classroom.

The British infant school approach probably will become the educational import to our shores to have the most impact since the graded Prussian school of the midnineteenth century. But whereas the graded school is a contradiction of how people naturally behave and learn, the new British infant school practices conform to and complement some of those self-evident truths about people and how they learn.

The British infant school approach, or the open classroom, is based on several important ideas about how learning occurs with which we concur. It also results in practices and consequences about which we have reservations.

Among the concepts of learning which it seeks to enhance are those espoused by the Italian educator and medical doctor, Maria Montessori, and the Swiss child psychologist, Jean Piaget. Montessori and Piaget found that most children learn abstract concepts best through concrete experiences that appeal primarily to their sense of touch.

Piaget emphasized that abstract concepts develop in a hierarchy of insights in a growth pattern common to all children. For example, more children will best learn addition by playing with blocks, beads, and other materials than they will by listening to an adult explain addition.

Children's purposes must be the basis for their learning. They must be able to experience learning rather than being instructed. They must be able to discover answers to their own questions. They must be able to investigate their world with their eyes and hands, and they must be able to learn some things by taste and smell.

In describing a classroom where her insights were put into practice, Dr. Montessori said, "Another important circumstance was the fact that the children were given special materials with which to work. They were attracted by these objects which perfected their sense perceptions, enabling them to analyze and facilitate their movements. These materials also taught them how to concentrate in a way that no vocal instruction ever could have done."

In the previous chapter we described a typical and exemplary American kindergarten where activities are directed primarily by the teacher and where many learning materials are so constructed and so arranged as to make them inappropriate, hard to get at, or uninviting for many children.

The teacher in the new British infant school approach is neither passive nor permissive. She is patient and forbearing, but she does not allow children to be either leaderless or rudderless. The successful teacher in the open school discovers that her role is to guide children's learning. She knows there are essential concepts and information that children should learn, and she keeps a careful record of each child's progress toward these goals.

The children in the open school also keep diaries in which they record their activities and experiences—what they have learned and how they have learned it.

Sometimes, a roomful of children will undertake a study of some major topic. In such instances, individuals and small groups of children will take pieces of the total project after planning sessions and consultation among themselves and with the teacher. The children's work is not haphazard or uncoordinated. They agree to schedules that carefully outline the work to be done, by whom, and by when.

Children in the open classroom direct their own activities, with the teacher serving as observer, guide, and counselor. The teacher is required to know what each child's abilities are, what his learning goals are, how far he has progressed in achieving those goals, and what kinds of experiences might be most appropriate for his continued progress. Thus fortified, the teacher is able to help children answer their questions about the activities in which they are engaged and able to guide children gently toward their learning goals if they have strayed or become lost.

The environment of the open classroom in the British infant school is most conducive to the personal investigation and individual learning desired.

There are no piano chords to tell all children to stop playing and get ready for the next activity.

There is no requirement that everybody work for a certain length of time at the tables in the center of the room. In fact, there are no tables in the center of the room, and the center of the room is hard to find in any case.

The open classroom is subdivided into learning centers for mathematics, reading and language development, science displays and little labs, where children learn alone, in pairs, and in groups. They learn from each other and from the wide variety of multisensory materials provided. They learn from their environment, and the environment has been created for children and not for adult housekeeping convenience.

The teacher and adult aides try not to intrude into this learning environment to instruct all of the children busily engaged in the hot pursuit of knowledge. The teacher and other adults work with individual children and with small groups as the children seek them out or as their offered services are accepted by the children.

As in the British infant school, the sign that might be posted for adults in our minischool would read: "Caution, Go Slow; Children at Work."

When children are at work in the environment of the open classroom, the air is alive with the sounds of learning. And the sounds are loud.

Children are asking, telling, and sharing; they express surprise, disappointment, joy, and occasionally antisocial behavior (which is gently handled). Children are in motion. They are building things up and tearing things down; there is pounding and molding, scraping and crashing; wood bangs against wood and metal clanks against metal; and occasionally child thuds against child. Visits to these classes dispel the myth of the stiff upper lip.

But we have some important reservations regarding the British infant school approach. For example, on-site visits to infant schools over a period of years reveals that while the British talk of mixing children of different ages in an open classroom, such "vertical grouping" occurs only some of the time. We would consider it necessary in the open classrooms of our minischool.

The rooms of the British infant school are tiny and cramped for the large numbers of children they contain. And the use of corridor space does not alleviate the tightness. The rooms—even the most newly constructed—have less floor space (approximately 600 square feet) than the typical classroom in the United States (approximately 750 square feet). And the number of children placed in the smaller room is about forty.

When the congestion is compounded by the addition of a wide variety of learning materials, the environment becomes very much like the opening hours of a very appealing bargain sale. The noise level in the rooms is very high, high even for the visitor who is impressed by the learning going on.

Teachers in the British open classrooms are both exuberant and tired at the same time. They tend to exhibit the compulsive enthusiasm common to converts to a cause, and this is wonderful to witness. The joyful climate in these schools is heady. Yet, the teachers sigh with relief when it comes their time to break for tea, or when they are spelled by aides.

What this all means to us is a confirmation of the truths about human learning. No one method, no one organization should be employed all day every day for all children and all teachers. But we would urge that children be permitted to enjoy the exuberant self-growth that comes from managing themselves in an active learning atmosphere.

We consider it unfortunate and unwise when people refer to the concepts and practices of the British infant school as The Method, The System, or The Way for American elementary schools.

In our view it is a good method, a good system, and a good way.

But just as teacher lecturing is not good for all children as a steady diet, so the British infant school approach is not good for all children all of the time.

And we would quickly add that the open classroom is probably not appropriate for some few children any of the time. There are youngsters who simply cannot learn in such an exciting, bustling environment, where self-motivation and self-direction play such important roles.

They need the security of a more quiet and more structured learning situation, where there is more adult direction (although not so much as to smother the child's particular zest for learning expressed in his own fashion). Hopefully, the goal would be to help such children grow until they are able to learn in the vigorous climate of an open classroom.

In the minischool there would be no need for any child to take the British infant school approach in large doses, or in any doses at all. But since exposure to this kind of learning approach would be good for most children some of the time, we would anticipate that a number of youngsters would spend some of their day or some of their week in an open classroom. But it might be for a major part of each day, for only an hour a day, or for two hours twice a week.

Exposure to the open classroom approach would be based on the child's needs and his ability to handle the enthusiasm generated by fast-paced learning. Again, the child's parents and counselor at the Community Guidance and Evaluation Center—in concert with teachers in the minischool—would help determine the child's participation in the British infant school setting.

The recognition that there is no best way for all children to learn is the keystone of the minischool—the foundation upon which all our proposed institutions are built. They stand or fall according to how well the foundation is poured in the first place.

If learners in our minischool for youngsters up to the age of eleven would not always be found in open classrooms modeled after the British infant school, where would they be?

Some of the children would spend some of their time at the minischool in solitary study, calling in a teacher or other children only as they need them. But solitary learning is not appropriate to any child all of the time. So, like everything else, the dosage will be measured to fit the prescription for individual children, a prescription written only after careful observation and with the avoidance of doctrinaire practices.

Some learning would take place in large groups, because some children learn best in large groups, and some children learn best that way most of the time.

For example, we have tended to shun mass responses, or recitation in unison, except when led by cheerleaders. Yet, there are children whose self-confidence is so weak that peer group chanting fortifies their sense of competency and social position. There are feelings of solidarity and unity to be derived from such joint expressions of learning.

While we have been constructing new models for learning, new forms based on the ways people act alone and together, we have been by implication describing the characteristics of the teachers needed by these new educational institutions.

Just as no one activity represents all learning for any child or all mankind, so no educational institution requires that every teacher be a leader or stimulator of all learning styles.

One of the handicaps the schools have lived with is the requirement that every teacher be a master of many techniques and a jack of all skills. Because most persons have had the good fortune to have learned from one such teacher in their lifetime, educators and laymen alike have lived with the illusion that good education would result in schools staffed solely by such superpeople.

We submit, therefore, that different forms of learning require teachers who are specialists in the particular forms.

There will be times in the minischool when many children would come together to hear a lecture, but lectures would not be assigned to all teachers in the minischool on a rotation basis. Those persons who talk to large groups would be those who have something to say and can say it very well. Talking to large groups effectively is a labor and an art not many people have mastered. We would want only those who have the skills to practice the art. The talks, of course, might not be given by teachers at all. They may be given by other adults or other students.

Children may come together from time to time for presentations that are not lectures. Other students may be learning by writing and presenting a play or puppet show, showing a movie or stack of slides; by singing, playing an instrument, or dancing. While the presenters learn, so might the audience. Teachers able to assist these processes could be superior specialists instead of today's somewhat overburdened generalists.

The minischool for youths aged twelve to eighteen would mix young people of different ages in a variety of learning patterns. Again, it is reasonable to expect that no student would spend all of his time at the minischool engaged in only one approach to learning.

But the minischool for youths would cater to the natural behavior of many persons of this age. That natural behavior is to associate in groups with persons who share like interests and goals.

Of course, we recognize that while most youths aspire to be a member of some youth group, a number never join one, some few by choice and more by rejection. Understanding this, we should emphasize that the learning approach we are about to describe is not going to serve everybody.

This learning method would involve self-organized and self-directed learning groups of twenty-five to fifty youths working with the guidance of one or more teacher-counselors. As in the British infant school approach, the teacher in this system would not dominate the learning—would not intrude except as it is desirable for the learners' sake.

A learning group would make an agreement, probably with the parent-teacher-student board operating the minischool. This agreement would spell out the learning goals of the group, the standards for admission of members, the established procedures for making decisions, how individual members plan to enhance their proficiencies, and how consequences of activities undertaken by the group in whole or in part will be measured and evaluated. Also, the roles of adult advisers would be outlined. And the group would be expected to describe what materials and funds might be needed, and how to account for those materials and funds.

The learning group would not be a shiftless, unmotivated mob lacking goals and not caring what the means to goals should be. Youths would organize learning groups that included people with whom they could feel comfortable most of the time as well as others with whom they might learn how to live. Learning groups would be prohibited from establishing negative admission standards.

Youths could not be excluded from a learning group because of race, religion, sex, father's occupation, or national origin.

For example, if a group of students were to form around a goal to study the local industrial park thoroughly and recommend changes and improvements to the community and to its appropriate agencies, then it might establish such admission standards as the following:

1. Membership is voluntary.
2. Members must be able to express a personal commitment or goal that is compatible with the group's goal. ("I want to determine whether the buildings are now making the best use of the land;" "I want to look into the impact of the park on nearby residential areas;" "I will find out what additional municipal services such as fire protection and sewage disposal might be needed if the park is expanded to include another twenty-five acres;" "Is this another move to drive out the poor?"
3. Members must be prepared to devote a minimum number of hours a week to the group's project.
4. Members should be willing to work in subgroups. Subgroups will report to the whole group on their work, such reports being given in any manner deemed appropriate by the subgroup (oral, dramatic, musical, filmed, recorded, and so on).

Discipline of individuals in a learning group should be accomplished by the actions of the group, with the assistance of adult counselors. Young people tend to overreact, and there might be calls for quick expulsion of members or other severe measures. Group ostracism can be painful; so, adult counseling would require empathy and firmness.

In the last three to five years, there have been attempts at free schools and colleges. Some, while they lasted, were in part creative models of what colleges and high schools lacked. They recaptured the joy of spontaneous learning, and they brought fresh relevance to the materials and modes of learning. They asked that some phase of an institution's energy be directed toward the removal or alleviation of the community's or the world's ills.

But the free schools and colleges have tended to fall apart. Many efforts have been destroyed from within by students who wanted the group to be used solely as an instrument for revolutionary change, who saw all education as a copout to an evil society. They have crumbled because in their anarchy decisions tended to be made by the most belligerent. They have collapsed because students could not distinguish between their needs and their whims, between deep interests and superficial and passing fancies. Most of all, they lacked central cohesion and money.

Accordingly, we have described the need for a formal agreement to validate the establishment of a learning group. It would generate a great deal of freedom, but it would contain safeguards against abuses.

Restraint always will bother some. But license to do one's own thing regardless of the consequences is an invitation to anarchy, not learning.

While the agreement would provide a framework in which the learning group would operate, it is not meant to be a shackle on freedom of operation. The members of the learning groups must be free, for instance, to make mistakes in the leadership they choose, in the goals they set out to achieve, and in the methods they select to evaluate their efforts.

In some groups, there will be leaders who are despots because other members of the group have allowed them to take charge. But teachers cannot rush in to erase the leadership and command the students to start all over again. The youths must learn—perhaps slowly and painfully—to be dissatisfied with their despot and to vote him out of his office.

Democracy is not learned in heaven. Then it's too late. Above all, we should have grasped that truth from what has happened in the schools of the past.

Students have been instructed in democracy in an essentially authoritarian atmosphere. They were permitted involvement only to the degree tolerated by a jealous institution. They were told how to be good citizens without being encouraged to establish goals, select means, and make formal judgments about outcomes.

Since the democratic process is fraught with risks, youths in their learning groups must be permitted to run some. It is part of their learning—a vital part. It is also a neglected fact that they need to learn how to make evaluations of how well or poorly they did.

The teacher/counselors to the learning groups would be on the lookout for youths who become isolated within the groups, for noncontribution, and for those who dominate excessively.

There would be nothing to prevent learning groups from accepting adults into their midst on the same basis as they do young people. For example, a group might organize that is devoted to writing and reading poetry.

Such a group might accept local poets and would-be poets from the college and from any other walk of life. The group might meet regularly in a coffeehouse of the members' own creation.

The life of a learning group might be a week or indefinitely. The duration of its existence would depend primarily on its goals and on the desires of its membership. The original agreement which established the group would contain a time estimate for its duration. If needed, it would be extended, or a new agreement could be written.

In the previous chapter we described another learning method for individuals and small groups. That is where students choose learning packages that enable them to proceed with their own programs, using the wide variety of materials in the package, the learning procedures suggested in the package, and any other appropriate materials and procedures the student might invent.

Also, some youths will need tutorial help some of the time; they will attend lectures and other large-group presentations some of the time; some students will learn some of the time from books that they read at home or in the library.

Students may learn in a variety of ways, and no one way is arbitrarily better than any other. We have already said that our Community Guidance and Evaluation Center would be concerned only with evaluating students' competencies, not with judging where or how they learned.

We would hope that society at large would adopt the same outlook.

- If a friend should eloquently recite Keats or Auden, does it matter where or when he came to love and learn them so well?
- If a prospective employee can demonstrate solutions to some of the more perplexing problems facing your company, does it matter where or how he learned to use higher mathematics to such good advantage?
- If a neighbor should come before the municipal governing council with an appropriate and realistic plan for cleaning the river, does it matter where he learned how to draft such a practical plan?

We have counted some of the ways of learning in the minischools. But there are alternatives to the minischools.

One such alternative is the Children's Neighborhood Learning Center. A center would operate under agreement for up to ten children in the age grouping of three to eleven (although a center might be just for children aged three to six, or for children aged nine to eleven).

The agreement would be between the administrative arm of the Education Assembly and a group of parents who have banded together to offer some opportunities for learning to their children in their own homes, or in other nonschool settings in the neighborhood.

The contract would call for the administrative arm of the Education Assembly to provide a center with a child development specialist to supervise the activities of the center under the direction of the board of parents.

The assembly also would arrange to provide learning materials, equipment, and tutors drawn from the volunteer ranks of teachers and older students.

The counselors and ombudsmen of the Community Guidance and Evaluation Center would work with the parents and their children to arrange educational experiences at the other institutions as desired and needed. Most children probably would not spend all of the day in a neighborhood center, but would visit the arts center, health center, and local minischool for part of the time.

The Community Guidance and Evaluation Center also would monitor the learning taking place in the neighborhood centers to insure that the children were developing in harmony with parental expectations.

Another alternative is the Neighborhood Reading Center.

These centers would be governed and staffed by community residents. They would serve community residents of all ages. They might be located in a storefront of 1,000 to 1,500 square feet, or they might be located in a mobile or fixed trailer.

Each center would be able to accommodate up to 500 individuals during a six-month period. The center's staff would consist of local residents working with the technical assistance of a trained reading specialist. Residents would be qualified for work in a neighborhood reading center if they wanted the job, needed the job, and could demonstrate literacy by reading and showing comprehension of the lead of a front-page story in the local daily newspaper.

The reading center would be organized into individual booths, because the reading instruction would be self-directed. Manufacturers of reading materials would be asked to supply self-instructional programs and the necessary materials for diagnosing reading proficiencies and deficiencies. The reading specialist assigned to the center would interpret diagnostic tests to help guide participants in their selection of instructional materials.

The reading center would be available to young children, older youth who never learned to read or didn't learn enough in school, and to adults in the same boat who now find it necessary or desirable to improve their reading ability. ("I need to read faster to get the job I want downtown.")

Of course, the reading center might also hold appeal for those who want to increase their reading speed and comprehension in order to read all they have to read in their job or want to read for their own enlightenment and recreation.

There is no stigma attached to the learning for drop-outs and adults, because it is private. There are no persons standing over a client's shoulder or at his side to point out that what he is learning is elementary, thereby embarrassing him and scaring him away from the learning experience.

The self-instructional materials would be so geared to each individual that they would take advantage of the dominance of his senses. For instance, if a young child learns best by feeling and touching, she would find a program in which she can instruct herself by touching letters and words, and so on.

Our preliminary estimates of total expenses indicate that a neighborhood reading center contained in 1,500 square feet could serve 1,000 individuals during the course of a year for less than $200 per person.

Another alternative is home instruction for individuals.

For years now schools have provided home instruction for handicapped and bedridden children. In the past twenty years, there have been refinements of such instruction through the use of telephone hookups with school classrooms and even television and radio on a limited basis. Such students also have had some tutoring at home.

We would make such home instruction available to all children and youth who might profit from it on a limited basis. We would not expect any healthy child to learn exclusively through home instruction. His counselor and ombudsman would make arrangements for his participation at the other institutions as such participation is in his best interests.

But for a part of every day or some days, some or all children of all ages might choose home instruction. Such home instruction might consist of nothing more than reading, but it might involve some or all of these activities:

1. playing a special learning cassette in a tape machine;
2. watching an educational film contained in a cassette inserted into the TV set;
3. conversing with scholars and other sources of information by telephone through special arrangement;
4. being tutored by another student or a teacher from the minischool.

A student taking some home instruction might be anyone, but particularly children and youths committed to heavy practice schedules in music, dance, or sports; children and youths committed to major writing, filmmaking, or composing; and children and youths who need more of the security of the home. Neighborhood groupings of four to ten could and would be encouraged to meet in homes of the participants.

We want to assure everyone that they should not worry about the complexity of so many diverse means and forms for education. Only school-management types who limit human learning to time schedules and places they can control need be disturbed. We seek educational forms that encourage different ways of learning, and primarily under the control of the learners.

The Education Assembly, concerned as it would be with providing education to all the people, might develop any number of programs for adults that do not tie in with the minischools or other institutions.

Again, this would be a major departure from what is offered today as adult education. Persons wishing to pursue learning find it necessary today to take most courses at the public schools on weeknights that are convenient to the school system.

Night adult education makes it difficult for mothers with small children to get out of the home, especially if the father is not home to sit with the children and baby-sitters in the area are too expensive, unreliable, or both.

For those who work at night—and this includes a great number of people—there is virtually no opportunity now to pursue education. The Education Assembly would be called upon to be exceptionally creative and relevant in designing programs suitable for adult members of the community. Of course, the institutions already described by us would be open to community residents during the day and night and on the weekends.

But there might be Adult Neighborhood Learning Centers operating out of homes similar to the learning centers conducted in homes for young children. The neighborhood adult groups would pick their own topics for study and contract with the administrative arm of the Education Assembly to provide materials and resource people.

For example, ten adults form a learning center that meets twice a week at 1 P.M. The group includes six women and four men. The men work odd shifts and 1 P.M. is the best time for all of them. Three of the women work 4 to 8 P.M. shifts, and the 1 P.M. time is best for them. The other women have arranged their schedules to be available at the appointed time. There are four married couples in the group.

The people have decided they would like to learn more about China, especially relations between China and the United States during the past twenty-five years. They contact the administrative arm of the Education Assembly and arrange for study aids including written materials, slides, and film strips. The assembly staff is also able to suggest names of several qualified residents of the community, including a professor at the nearby university, who would be available to meet with the group from time to time. The assembly also suggests to the group that it communicate with the Community Guidance and Evaluation Center to arrange for testing if members of the group are interested. Only two of the group decide they would like to have their knowledge of Chinese affairs tested after they complete the unit.

Some adult learning centers would work with learning packages available at the minischools. And the minischools would be open for adult use during the day and night and on weekends. We already have indicated the minischools would invite attendance by adults. We see learning groups consisting of all adolescents, all adults, and a shared membership. The important concept governing their organization is their new doctrinaire openness.

Of course, groups of families might organize into a Family Neighborhood Center, where adults, children, and youths work cooperatively on study units and learning packages of their own choosing. The Guidance and Evaluation Center would monitor such endeavors and provide testing services as needed.

The Education Assembly might want to initiate field service seminars in child care and training for mothers on a neighborhood basis. The program might be modeled after the field services established many years ago to help rural housewives learn homemaking.

A field service agent would visit small groups of mothers in a home or other nonschool setting on a regular basis. She would bring pamphlets, films, records, demonstration equipment, and whatever other learning materials are necessary.

Field service seminars also might be arranged to train women to provide in their homes what is being called foster day care for children of working mothers.

In big cities across the land there are thousands of mothers who take their children to a nearby apartment or house to spend the day while they go off to jobs. In many situations, the children are placed before a television set for the day and given a lunch consisting of a piece of bread and some baloney, or a hot dog.

A number of attempts are being made now to provide some form of foster day care. Unfortunately, most of them are on a small scale, and nearly all of them are outside the framework, recognition, and sanction of organized education. Private industry is pioneering in some areas and welfare agencies in others. Along with our repeated call for volunteer labor in many of our proposed educational forms, there is a need for official sanction and financial stability. Hence, the Education Assembly should be stimulating and supportive in this field.

The Education Assembly might determine there is a need for a field service agent to train individuals to operate foster day care centers in their home. Such trained surrogate parents could be fortified with packets of materials for child play provided by the educational authority.

We have counted some of the ways and settings in which children, youths, and adults might learn. But our listing is just a beginning. We would expect the Education Assembly, in cooperation with the staffs of the major institutions under its jurisdiction, to create a great variety of programs to meet the educational needs and desires of the people served by the assembly.

Freed from the restriction of thinking only about courses of instruction in buildings called schools, the Education Assembly would be under the extraordinary pressures of a society hungry for new learning, dissatisfied with old forms and older systems, and eager for fresh thinking.

Throughout the discussion of our new Design for Education, we have consistently made the point that people would not learn in one way and in one place. Learning would happen in a wide variety of locations and by means not even imagined today.

Children and youths would divide their time between minischool and arts center, between home instruction and health center, between learning packages and learning groups, between open classroom and neighborhood reading center, between volunteer service and work experience, between private instruction in the arts and individual or group learning expeditions to the human and material resources of the community.

And we see no reason why some children should not continue to spend some of their day or week taking instruction at St. Leo's Roman Catholic Church, the Evangelical Lutheran Church, or Temple Emmanuel, or from Buddhists and Black Muslims.

We see no objection to children and youths performing volunteer service or engaging in work experiences in local religious institutions. Why shouldn't a girl volunteer time at a day care center operated by the United Methodist Church as well as at the municipal hospital's pediatrics ward? Why shouldn't a young man who expects to train for ministry to the urban poor work through a church scholarship under the tutelage of a priest ministering to the urban poor?

The heated debate over public assistance to private institutions might be cooled if society were to adopt our vision and that of our proposed Education Assembly. Then, it would see individuals choosing where they will learn and how they will learn instead of individuals simply making choices between church school and P.S. 21.

Today, shared time is an argumentative political question because it is one form of implied subsidy to church-sponsored schools. But the institutions sponsored by our Education Assembly would be open to all. There would no longer be a question of shared time for some, because everyone could share among diverse settings for learning, service, and work, and among widely varied paths to learning.

Epilogue:

A Way to Begin

OUR DESIGN FOR COMMUNITY EDUCATION restores old truths about learning in new educational forms, and offers plain arguments and common sense.

Thomas Paine hoped his little pamphlet of common sense would rouse the American people into severing their ties with a government that no longer served them well. We hope our book—our plan for action—will so rouse the American people that they will sever their ties with the old educational institutions that no longer serve them well—the school board, the graded school, and its malfunctioning appendages.

War was waged to insure the nation's independence, but the United States of America was conceived and shaped in sober convention. We don't call for violent overthrow of the schools, but we do call for community conventions from coast to coast and border to border to convert the words on these pages—the blueprint—into a lively system that offers learning to the people according to how they want it, where they want it, and when they want it.

In the best American tradition, the people could be called together to examine the present status of education in their community and to consider how our Design for Community Education might better serve the educational needs of all of the people in the future.

A community convention should consider how education in the community now stacks up against education as it could be made

174

available through the series of new institutions we propose. This
will mean asking some hard questions.

- Is the board of education *really* representative of the people
  it serves, and does it confine itself to considering and passing
  legislation that makes education available and relevant to
  everybody?
- Is the emphasis now on instruction of students in grades
  in schools? Should it be on learning by individuals in a
  variety of settings?
- Are the arts an integral part of the life of the community,
  or are they mainly subjects to be taught in school and to
  be engaged in and enjoyed by a very few residents?
- Do the school system's guidance and counseling offices
  serve parents and their children and other residents of the
  community as preferred clients? Should they?
- Does the educational program need regular and objective
  evaluation? Is it getting it now?
- Are all young people aged fourteen to eighteen now able
  to engage in volunteer service and work experiences in
  the community and its environs? Should they have such
  opportunities?

A convention should not be called by the board of education,
the administration of the school system, or the teachers' union.
All of these parties should be active participants in the deliberations,
but it would be awkward for them and probably unproductive for
the community if they acted as sponsors.

An institution may risk examination by outsiders—even a critical
look—but it would be unnatural for it to allow the invited guests
to follow the examination with a decision to change the institution
radically or even to replace it.

A convention might be called by an ad hoc coalition of community organizations, by the federation of PTAs, by the League
of Women Voters, by the community's governing body, or by the
chamber of commerce.

Meetings of the convention should be open to all residents of the community, but there should be representation from at least the following segments of the community: the municipal governing body, political parties, the board of education, the school administration, teachers' organizations, young people aged fourteen to eighteen, churches and other religious organizations, labor unions, ethnic and racial minorities, community organizations (from the Rotary Club to the militant civil rights group), and school organizations (such as the PTA).

The participants definitely should include medical and health professionals, lawyers, people involved in the community's cultural endeavors, finance specialists, architects, and building contractors.

Before all of these people come together, the sponsor(s) of the convention might call upon a group of scholars in education, the arts, and economics to make an outside audit of the state of local education. The results of such an audit should be in the hands of the people before the convention gets underway.

Using the outside audit as its foundation, the convention could begin its examination of education in the community as it is and as it should and can be. Taking their lead from this book, the convention should not limit its study to what is, or can be, offered only in schools and through established curricula and learning methods.

When the convention has answered most of the hard questions, it should be ready to make decisions and authorize action. At this stage, it should elect a steering committee to carry out its directives.

As it is important for all elements and interests in the community to be represented at the convention, they also should have representation on the steering committee—perhaps in fewer numbers. The steering committee should be a political body prepared to take whatever steps are authorized by the convention.

Suppose the convention should decide that the present seven-member board of education should be superseded by a twenty-five-member Education Assembly over a two-year period.

The steering committee should begin an immediate study of existing voting districts. The committee will want to know, for example, whether people elected to the Education Assembly from the existing districts would be representative of all the people. Perhaps some districts were gerrymandered in the past to preserve power for some party, some organization, some ethnic or religious group, or some individual.

The committee should draft an organizational plan for the Education Assembly. The plan should detail how assembly members would be elected, how long they would serve, how the assembly would conduct its business, and what kind of executive arm it needs.

It also may be necessary for the committee (which should include a lawyer or two) to draft a bill for the state legislature which would enable the community to elect an assembly in place of its board of education. Hopefully, other communities would be taking similar steps in support of such enabling legislation. The law sought should not *require* assemblies, but should permit communities to adopt such a form of educational governance.

We anticipate wide support for the convention and the decisions it might make to implement some or all of our Design for Community Education. Of course, we are not so naive as to suppose there will be unanimous support, or that there will not be opposition from some persons whose own interests would not be best served by the plan. However, experience also demonstrates that support often is found among those that had been prejudged as opponents.

- The local governing body should be among the supporters, if for no other reason than that a more representative education body would have to have broad community support for raising taxes. For the mayor or councilman who now feels that the people hold him most responsible for rising taxes, a truly representative education body should be welcome.
- Speaking of taxes, the people's investment in our Design for Community Education would be a far cry from today's school tax. No longer would taxpayers be paying just to support schools for children and youths. They would be paying to support education for residents of all ages—in-

cluding themselves—in a variety of settings throughout the community. The slogan "Support Your Schools for the Children's Sake," would be replaced by the slogan "Support Education for Everybody's Sake, Including Yours."

● The concept of a Community Guidance and Evaluation Center to provide an impartial and expert audit of education in the community might be feared by some professional educators, but it should appeal strongly to all those who expect and deserve a fair return on their investment. And we talk not only of the investment of money, but more important, the investment of lives. There are thousands of parents today who feel their lives and their children's lives have been unfulfilled because of what didn't happen in school.

● Those persons and groups who want students, parents, and other community residents to help determine what kind of education will be available and how it will be administered should be supporters. Through our Design for Community Education, students, parents, and other community residents would not simply be tolerated as occasional advisers; they would not be merely the objects of paternalism. They would be in charge of what matters.

● Of course, parents should be supportive of the Design for Community Education. It would give them the opportunity—perhaps for the first time—to feel that education was tailored to suit their children. And they and their children would have counselors and ombudsmen who treat them as preferred clients, because that's what they are.

● Leaders of business, unions, and the professions should be supporters. They should be able to see immediately the advantages of the Career Education Center, where interested students under competent supervision would seek to learn from and contribute to a wide range of occupations.

● Because education in all of its many forms would be available to adults during the day as well as at night, our Design for Community Education should have appeal to persons who work at night and now enjoy precious few opportunities to pursue learning.

● The older residents of the community, those whose children are now grown and scattered, should have a stake in the Design for Community Education. A myriad of opportunities to learn and create would be available to them in lively settings, where people of other generations would treat them as fellow learners and artists. They would not be objects of charity and paternalism, nor would they be invited as unpaid baby-sitters. The enthusiasm for work and play could be genuine and rewarding, and not a kind of synthetic enthusiasm generated by a skillful activities director at an enclave for retired people.

The Design for Community Education is ambitious, but its price tag should not deter its implementation.

It is not possible to make accurate cost comparisons between education today and education as it could be tomorrow through our series of new institutions. But there are several important points to be made.

The institutions we propose would be open during the day, at night and on weekends—and all year long. Today's schools, on the other hand, generally are closed two-thirds of the day during the week, closed throughout the weekend, and mostly closed for the summer.

And because learning schedules for everybody would be exceedingly flexible, the facilities we plan would be capable of much greater utilization—perhaps as much as 40 to 50 percent more—than today's schools. For example, children and youths typically would spend only two or three hours a day in a minischool, thereby allowing a great many more individuals to use the facilities than would be possible if each person were required to be in school from 8:30 A.M. to 2:30 P.M.

Many of the institutions we have proposed do not require the community to go out and build new buildings immediately, although long-range planning for some new facilities should be undertaken at the outset.

The Family Health Center we have proposed could utilize space now occupied in a number of schools by a gymnasium, locker room, and nurse's office. Except that probably the gymnasium and locker room used now by the varsity basketball team should be turned over to the municipal recreation authority along with the varsity football stadium and most of the baseball diamonds.

The Community Arts Center could get started in existing buildings with some interior renovations. The Career Education Center does not require a lot of space to help place students in service jobs and work experiences.

Our proposed minischools certainly could operate out of existing school buildings, with some modifications.

The Education Assembly could begin operations by taking over a cluster of classrooms for its meetings and for administrative offices.

The Community Guidance and Evaluation Center probably should be kept away from the other institutions. We don't want to risk the center's domination by institutions it is supposed to evaluate. We don't want to risk the center's staff giving their allegiance to employees of other institutions instead of to the center's preferred clients.

A building to house the Community Guidance and Evaluation Center temporarily might be found in the community. But if education officials are contemplating constructing a new school, it might be able to erect a new guidance and evaluation center instead—and for considerably less money. The school possibly would not be needed because of the increased utilization of existing facilities already mentioned.

But when that first new building is constructed to house one of our proposed new institutions, it should be the most beautiful and most functional building in town. We hope education assemblies will find architects whose imaginations range beyond cement block or brick boxes. We're not advocating exceptionally expensive buildings, just exceptional buildings—buildings designed to lift the spirit as well as to suit exactly the needs for which they are intended.

We visualize much more volunteer service to our new institutions than is now given to the schools.

It is interesting to note today, for example, how many young people and adults devote time in a great variety of ways to their community hospital, but how few young people and adults devote time to their schools. If they are volunteers in the schools, often they are restricted to serving as aides in the library.

We would anticipate adults and young people serving as volunteers in our proposed institutions in many different capacities. For example, they could be tutors, aides in the open classrooms of minischools for younger children, assistant counselors to learning groups in the minischools for older students, in charge of materials at the arts center, aides to the staff of the health center, and helpers in the libraries and museums.

While there might be some savings derived from such volunteer service, the real purpose of encouraging people to devote a little time to their institutions is to allow them the privilege of giving of themselves and being greatly satisfied and rewarded by the act.

Probably in no other country of the world is volunteer service so commonplace as in the United States. Unfortunately, not much of it has been given to education, largely because in the past it was frequently not welcomed by a suspicious institution. Our institutions not only would welcome volunteer services offered, they would actively seek out such assistance.

We cannot provide a manual to show America how to implement our Design for Community Education in twenty-five easy steps, accompanied by simple-to-follow diagrams. We cannot say it will cost just so many dollars to do this piece of the design or that piece.

But that has not been our purpose in these pages. Our purpose has been to demonstrate how and why the present institutions for education—the school board, the graded school, and its many appendages—cannot serve the educational needs of individuals of any age, no matter how many innovations and precious dollars we pump into them.

The institutions as now constituted compel certain behaviors and attitudes on the part of those who must live by their rules.

We propose to replace the school board and the graded and appended school for mass instruction of boys and girls with a series of new institutions to encourage learning by individuals of all ages. And institutions would be added to or subtracted from as the learning needs of the community change.

To paraphrase Lord Acton, the eminent British historian and philosopher, speaking of his countrymen: "We English venerate the forms of freedom without an awareness of the substance behind the forms. We hold as an ideal the concept of pure democracy, but in a pure democracy there is no relief from the tyranny of the majority. We hold graft to be a universal evil, but under tyranny, graft is the only form of relief."

Similarly, we Americans have for too long assumed that a form for education called a school promoted and insured learning. If it once did, it no longer does.

America has for more than a century venerated the public school as The Only Way to education. But it is not the only way; in its form of long standing it is no longer even a good way. The venerated form has, in fact, been a straitjacket on the learning and creativeness of children and their teachers over the years. It has compelled behaviors from teachers and children inimicable to ancient truths and common sense about learning.

In today's graded and appended school there can be no genuine and long-lasting relief from those negative behaviors, from that kind of teaching that makes learning difficult.

Relief can come—will come—only if we can muster the courage and the strong will to replace the form, the institution, the school.

We have offered a list of alternative new forms for education to encourage rather than inhibit learning.

The design of institutions to suit his purposes is the oldest of man's activities—and the newest of man's sciences. We offer our Design for Community Education as a way—a good way—to serve man's need to learn about himself and his world.

Index